FINGER TIPS

FINGER TIPS

Professional Manicurists' Techniques for Beautiful Hands and Feet

By Elisa Ferri
with
Mary-Ellen Siegel

Illustrations by Rex
Design by Tom Stvan

Clarkson N. Potter, Inc./Publishers
DISTRIBUTED BY CROWN PUBLISHERS, INC., NEW YORK

ACKNOWLEDGMENTS

The following people gave freely of their time and expertise, reading portions of the manuscript and making valuable suggestions:

Daniel Carucci, M.D.
Joel Kassimir, M.D.
Irene Prisco
Barry Weinbaum
Eric Weinstein, D.P.M.

Pam Krauss's encouragement, suggestions, and assistance are enormously appreciated. Rex's contribution was enormous. We are grateful to Connie Clausen and Guy Kettelhack for bringing us all together.

ALSO BY MARY-ELLEN SIEGEL

Her Way

What Every Man Should Know About His Prostate (coauthored with Monroe E. Greenberger, M.D.)

More Than a Friend: Dogs with a Purpose (coauthored with Hermine M. Koplin)

Reversing Hair Loss

The Cancer Patient's Handbook

The Nanny Connection (coauthored with O. Robin Sweet)

Published by Clarkson N. Potter, Inc., 225 Park Avenue South, New York, New York 10003 and represented in Canada by the Canadian MANDA Group.

CLARKSON N. POTTER, POTTER, and colophon are trademarks of Clarkson N. Potter, Inc.

Manufactured in the United States of America

Library of Congress Cataloging-in-Publication Data

Ferri, Elisa.
    Finger tips.
    1. Nails (Anatomy)—Care and hygiene.   2. Manicuring.
I. Siegel, Mary-Ellen.   II. Title.
RL94.F47   1988   646.7'27   87-32680
ISBN 0-517-56827-6 (pbk.)

10 9 8 7 6 5 4 3 2 1

First Edition

To our mothers:
Marie Bellingreri, whose beauty and grace is
always an inspiration; and Miriam Baum
Greenberger, whose radiance will live forever.

CONTENTS

INTRODUCTION

Mother was right when she said that first impressions were lasting ones. Extended hands are calling cards; a well-groomed one can open doors— and a neglected, unattractive one can close them. Most women wouldn't dream of going out without combing their hair and putting on a dash of makeup—but it's surprising how many forget to give their hands and nails the same care and attention.

At one time beautiful hands and nails were the exclusive domain of the idle rich; businesswomen and mothers settled for plain and simple nails. But every woman can have graceful, elegant hands—not just the executive who has her mail opened and her phones dialed for her, but the woman who works with her hands in and out of the home. All it requires is a commitment of forty-five uninterrupted minutes a week and remembering to follow my tips the rest of the time.

Your feet can be as pampered and well-cared for as your hands, and *Finger Tips* tells you how. The men in your life, whether their tools are pencils, computers, scalpels, or hammers and saws, can have well-groomed hands too.

The following pages contain the same tips I have been sharing with my private and corporate clients for more than twelve years, the women who visited the salon where I first started out and the celebrities and models I work with today.

Whether these women are suburban housewives or international personalities, they all use their hands; they rinse out their drip-dries in hotels, pack suitcases, and fix stuck zippers. They can't depend on having someone handy to fasten those out-of-reach snaps and buttons. Nor do they always have a professional manicurist within easy reach, so they need to know how to keep their nails and hands beautiful.

Beautiful hands begin with healthy nails and you *can* achieve that goal. In the pages that follow you will learn how to prevent split and broken nails, how to keep polish fresh-looking for days, and how to correct any problems that may arise. You will find out how to make nice nails look nicer and how to create special looks for important occasions.

I will discuss the equipment you need to keep your nails beautiful; the shapes of nails; how, when, and where to do your nails; and the *right* way to do them. Choosing a color is important, and I'll explain how to determine which ones are right for you. You will learn to do repairs and even extensions just as the salons do.

And even if you *do* decide to have an occasional professional manicure, you will be able to do your own nails beautifully between appointments, and communicate more effectively with your manicurist. But there's really no reason to spend a fortune on manicures or be at the mercy of the salon's schedule when everything you need to know in order to have beautiful nails is right in your own hands!

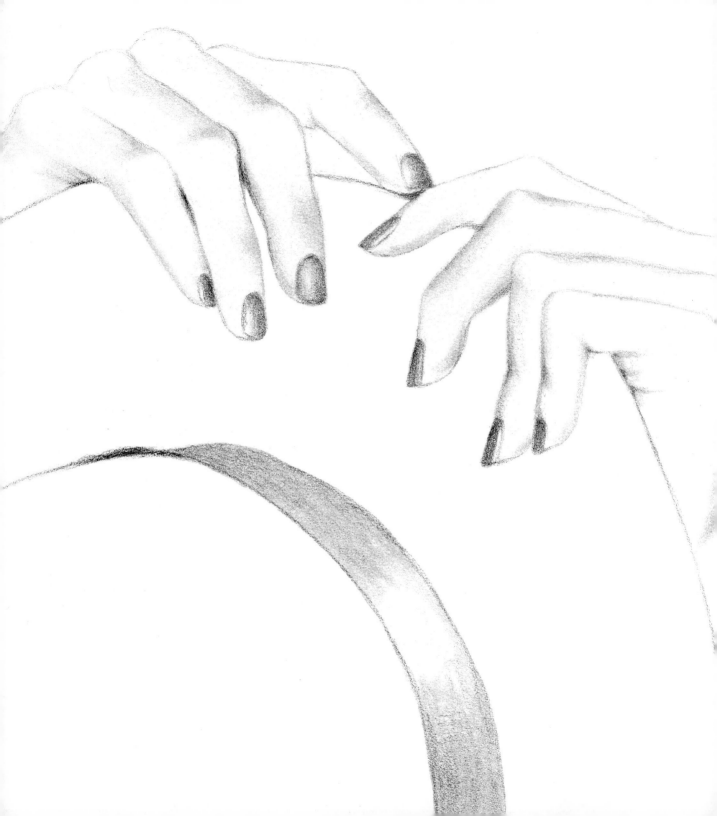

1 HEALTHY HANDS AND NAILS

Most of us have healthy nails; keeping them in their prime is not a complicated or time-consuming task. For the most part, it really just involves common sense. Maintaining a healthy diet and protecting nails from the elements are basic to having beautiful nails.

WHAT ARE NAILS MADE OF?

Nails, like hair, are really extensions of the skin and are made up of a tough protein called keratin. That which we call a *nail* really consists of many parts, the nail plate (the part you file and polish) being the part that is visible. Like hair, the nail plate does not contain any living cells; it is whitish in color, but looks pink because the nail bed on which it rests is supplied with blood vessels, which provide for nail growth. The nail bed also contains nerves.

The nail plate extends outward from the root, under the *lunula* (the whitish-half moon at the base of the nail) to the fingertip or, as it is called, the *free edge* of the nail. The lunula is more visible in some people than others. Under this root there are a group of cells called the *matrix*. Injury to the matrix—a nail disorder, severe malnutrition, or other illness—can slow down the growth of the nails. Trauma, such as catching your finger in a door, can lead to temporary or even permanent loss of a nail.

Surrounding and overlapping the nail is the *cuticle*. Composed of dead skin cells, the cuticle has the important function of keeping out dirt and bacteria. The *eponychium*, an extension of the cuticle at the base of the nail, partly overlaps the lunula. This is the area that is sometimes pushed backward and, under some circumstances, trimmed during a manicure.

NAIL GROWTH

Unlike hair, which goes through cycles of growth, rest, and loss, nails grow continuously. New growth starts at the matrix and moves forward beyond the fingertip. Rates of growth vary among individuals and are determined by age as well as health factors; growth slows down as we get older, but the average adult's nails grow about one-eighth of an inch a month. This may not sound like much, but if you hold a ruler up to your hand you will see you can have significant growth in a month or two. Toenails grow only one-third to one-half as fast as fingernails. They are thicker, harder, and less vulnerable to splitting and breakage.

Nails grow faster just before menstruation, during pregnancy, and during warm weather. A nail that has been injured will grow faster during the recovery period. Many people say that the nails on their dominant hand grow faster, and pianists and typists seem to have a speedier nail growth than others. This is probably because the pressure on the fingertip pad increases circulation.

BASIC CARE OF HANDS AND NAILS

Most dermatologists agree that it is far easier to protect nails than it is to treat them. The worst enemies of your hands and nails are the elements—especially water—chemicals, and your own

Lunula

Free edge

Nail plate

Cuticle

carelessness. Dishwater, or any water for that matter, goes quickly through the nail, causing it to swell. Once you remove your hands from water, the nails dry out and shrink, weakening their structure and making them prone to breakage, especially when this occurs repeatedly.

One of the best defenses against stained, chipped, and dried-out nails is gloves, and you should outfit yourself with a whole wardrobe of them. Whenever you immerse your hands in water for prolonged periods, or use strong chemicals for even a few minutes, wear protective gloves. I like the kind with cotton lining (the heavy blue ones are really good) because they don't radiate as much heat or trap the moisture inside as others tend to do. Use them for the following:
- scrubbing pots and pans
- doing hand laundry
- heavy cleaning
- using chemicals such as ammonia or cleansing powders

For tasks that require more agility than the heavy gloves allow (such as washing your grandmother's tea cups and crystal), try vinyl surgical gloves, available in most pharmacies. Some surgical gloves comes with talc inside to make them easier to slip on, or you can sprinkle some talc in yourself; buy them in your precise glove size for a good fit. Avoid extremely hot water, which creates heat and moisture inside the glove. And don't think you'll be clumsy in surgical gloves; if neurosurgeons and ophthalmologists can function with them, so can you!

Wear surgical gloves for the following:
- washing delicate china and crystal
- coloring your hair (they're much better than the flimsy plastic ones that come with the hair product)
- handling fish, garlic, or onions (these are all irritants to the skin and some of them can stain or dry out your hands and nails)

Gardening gloves will protect your hands from scrapes and nicks and from staining, especially under the nails. They also reduce nail breakage. Use them when you:
- work outside
- repot house plants

Finally, never, never go out in the cold without gloves.

Wash your hands as carefully as you do your face, using a mild, superfatted soap. Dermatologists recommend Dove because it doesn't strip off the normal acid mantle of the skin as do typical alkaline soaps. Always pat your hands dry after washing, rather than rubbing them. Once in a while use a facial mask or scrub on your hands (an oatmeal scrub is nice) to slough off dead skin and tighten pores.

Each time your hands have been in water, follow with hand cream or lotion. Keep jars of hand cream next to your bed, on your desk, in the kitchen, with your garden supplies, next to the washing machine, as well as in the bathroom. Rub it in well, and often; don't be stingy with it. Be sure that you work the lotion into the cuticles too. (Blot the palms of your hands with tissues to avoid stickiness.)

SPECIAL TIP: If your hands are really chapped, try this: Leave them slightly damp after washing, apply lotion (to add moisture to skin), and then put on a pair of surgical gloves for an hour or two.

There is no need to buy expensive hand creams since most of them work the same way. The more modestly priced are often fragrance-free; if they contain aloe and vitamin E (good for healing) they will be especially helpful. At night you can use petroleum jelly (or pure lanolin if you're not allergic to it); cover with white cotton gloves to protect your bed linens and to help hold the moisturizer on your skin.

SPECIAL TIP: When you're outdoors in the sun for extended periods, use a sunscreen on your hands as well as your face to prevent premature aging and the possibility of skin cancers.

Think before you act! Taking the time to locate a staple remover or screwdriver instead of using your fingernails can make the difference between looking like a hard laborer and a lady of leisure, even if you aren't either.

Contrary to belief, a manicure is not just "makeup" for your nails. It offers protection to your hands and nails.

You wouldn't put a can of paint or a pot of coffee on your good mahogany table without a protector; treat your nails just as kindly and keep a clear base coat on them even if you don't have time for a full manicure. Don't overdo things; more isn't better, so don't give yourself biweekly or triweekly manicures. Don't use nail polish remover more than once every five days (even the nonacetone ones are drying), and don't cut your cuticles, because this can lead to infections.

SPECIAL TIP: Always act as if your nails are still wet from a manicure at the most expensive salon in town; you'll respect them and treat them kindly.

WHAT CAN GO WRONG

Any number of problems can occur in and around the nails, and often it is difficult to determine the exact diagnosis or cause. Many conditions can be caused by environmental factors as well as health concerns. When you do notice a nail problem, it is important to consult a dermatologist to determine its precise cause.

For instance, the condition where nails separate from the nail bed (onycholysis) beginning at the free edge may be caused by solvents or base coats containing formaldehyde or from depilatories. Separation can also result from prolonged use of sculptured or bonded nails, particularly if portions of the nail plate adhere to the false nail when you remove it. It is also possible to have a severe allergic reaction to the glues used in attaching some of these nails. Other causes of nail separation may be psoriasis, infections, or other allergies.

When problems do occur, they generally fall into one of these categories:
- dermatological conditions
- reactions of nails to drugs taken internally, such as antibiotics, chemotherapy, and antimalarial drugs

ROLE OF DIET AND VITAMINS

Unless you are suffering from a gross vitamin deficiency, additional vitamins will not cure nail problems. Never take more than the recommended doses of vitamins A, D, or E (all of which have been touted as good for the nails) without a physician's approval. Toxicity is often an unwanted and unanticipated side effect. Vitamin D toxicity, for instance, can lead to overly thick nails. However, vitamin E, applied topically either in ointment form or by piercing a capsule and spreading the contents over the nails, can be helpful, though physicians warn against the indiscriminate use of topical vitamin E, which can cause allergies.

Many women wonder if a low-cholesterol diet will be detrimental to their nails. The answer: The body makes enough cholesterol to care for your nails, so you can safely reduce your intake.

What about megadoses of calcium? According to physicians the calcium in a healthy diet or in the supplement recommended to both pre- and post-menopausal women is all that healthy nails need. Excessive doses of calcium can lead to kidney stones.

- reactions to local or topical agents, such as cosmetics, ointments, soaps, etc.
- trauma
- organisms such as bacteria, fungi, or viruses
- medical conditions, such as coronary disease, auto-immune diseases, anemia
- tumors (benign or malignant)

In many cases, nail conditions will correct themselves when the underlying cause is corrected. Some can easily be remedied at home, but others need the attention of a physician who can diagnose the problem, determining if the cause is internal or external. Antifungal, antibiotic, or cortisone medications may be prescribed to be taken internally or applied topically. (Diabetics should see a physician for even a minor infection, and should never let a nonmedical person attempt to cut their cuticles.) Following are some of the most common nail ailments and their causes.

DISCOLOR-ATION

Nails are like sponges; they can absorb color from nail polishes and hardeners, dyes, carbon paper, typewriter and printer ribbons, tea, garlic, bleach, freckle cream, suntan lotions, nicotine—the list is almost endless. Infections, drugs taken internally, and a number of diseases can also cause discoloration of the nails. The tetracyclines (which are photosensitive), in particular, can change nail color in conjunction with sun exposure.

Brown nails are usually directly related to contact with certain chemicals found in household or gardening supplies or hair dyes. Wear protective gloves when handling chemicals; if you keep a pair in all the places where you are likely to be handling chemicals, even for a few minutes, you will be less tempted to go without them.

OCCUPATIONAL HAZARDS

People in certain occupations are prone to nail problems. Hairdressers and barbers whose hands are in water a great deal and who use nonabsorbable materials such as bristles; gardeners or florists who handle daffodils, hyacinths, or tulips (which contain specific irritants); dentists, dental, medical, or photographic technicians, and others who handle solutions and chemicals, or any kind of varnishes, dyes, or chromium salts, insecticides, or formaldehydes are all likely candidates for contact dermatitis. This is a general term that describes inflammation and irritation (and sometimes itching or pain) from an external cause. Nonprescription cortisone cream can be helpful; use as directed and if there's no improvement a dermatologist should be consulted.

Manual laborers, those who use powerful vibrating tools, potters, and key punch operators all may suffer fractured or broken nail plates.

Cooks, dishwashers, homemakers, swimmers, bartenders, and many health-care workers, including physicians and nurses, are all subject to water-logging, which can lead to split, broken, and weak nails.

Occasionally nails turn brown in reaction to chemotherapy, other drugs, or diseases.

Yellow nails are usually directly related to chemical or nicotine contact. Fungus can cause this; so can long-time use of tetracycline. If you have used dark nail polish without first applying a good base coat, your nails may have become stained and look "yellowish." If this happens, go without polish for a few days and rub the nail plate with lemon juice. To prevent yellowing, always use a ridge filler as a base coat before polishing.

Sometimes yellow nails can be traced to a blood disorder, diabetes, lung or thyroid disease, rheumatoid arthritis, or accumulation of lymph fluid.

Bluish nails may just be the result of chemical contact, or due to trauma or hemorrhage under the nail. Blue-black or gray nails sometimes follow prolonged stress, which interferes with nail formation. If all the nails are blue, it may be the result of insufficient circulation or a cardiac condition.

Green nails are just what they appear to be: moldy. Bacterial infections such as these develop from lack of proper hygiene. I'm going to be very direct here—some people are just plain lazy! Moldy nails can develop in women who begin with sculptured nails or nail wraps, then fail to maintain them, keep them clean and dry, and see their manicurists *immediately* if a separation develops between the artificial and natural nail. If the client postpones seeking attention, the gap will begin to collect dirt, food particles, and moisture, which leads to green nails. Usually if the artificial nail is removed when trouble arises, and the natural nail is kept clean and very dry with a twice-daily application of an over-the-counter antibiotic cream, the green will grow out, leaving healthy pink nail. If improvement is not rapid, a dermatologist should be consulted.

Black spots on nails are coagulated blood caused by small hemorrhages. Usually this follows minor traumas that you may not have even noticed; catching your finger in a suitcase, for instance. The spots will grow out as the nail grows, unless the damage was done to the base of the nail. Then, especially if it was a more serious trauma (the kind you are unlikely to forget), the nail will loosen and fall off.

A persistent black spot, not ascribed to a trauma, that does not seem to be growing out should be seen by a physician, preferably a dermatologist, to be sure it is not something more serious, such as a malignant melanoma. Dark streaks may be caused by adrenal gland insufficiency and should be checked with your physician.

White spots, flecks, and ridges (see illustration, page 8) are harmless, and usually develop from trauma. They will grow out as the nail grows. Totally opaque, white, or half-white nails can be hereditary, or may be associated with severe vitamin deficiency or kidney or liver disease.

Discoloration of nails that cannot be attributed to any known cause should be brought to the attention of a physician.

PROBLEMS WITH TEXTURE

Peeling nails may be caused by extreme dryness or filing or trimming them straight across rather than following their natural curve. Peeling off old nail polish may take the nail with it, especially if nails are already soft, weak, or brittle. Use a good nail hardener to strengthen nails and a moisturizer with vitamin E oil or pure lanolin to prevent nail layers from separating and peeling.

Vertical ridges often begin to develop around age forty, and are no cause for concern. Raynaud's disease, a condition in which there is a loss of circulation resulting in cold fingers, can cause these ridges at any age.

Horizontal ridges can occur from injury or from a too-vigorous manicure, but a virus, fever, or kidney or liver disease can also cause them. Ridge-filler (page 17), followed by colored polish, will help any nails with ridges look much better.

Brittleness, which may cause nails to split, is a frequent consequence of aging. At any age, brittleness can be caused by dryness and exposure to detergents, cleansers, and irritating chemicals, and too frequent use of nail polish remover, cuticle softeners and removers, nail hardeners, and undercoats, as well as injuries to the fingernails.

Prolonged immersion in water will increase the moisture content of the normal nail plate, making nails softer. Just as your skin gets chapped, nails become brittle, which then causes them to split and crack.

Sometimes the tendency to develop brittle nails is hereditary, so if this is your legacy be sure to take extra precautions. Keep your nails shorter to avoid breakage, which can lead to injuries on the nail bed. File them regularly, because smooth nails are not as likely to catch on things. Very brittle nails should be clipped *after* soaking rather than before, to prevent injury.

More than others, those with brittle nails need to be very conscientious about using lotions and creams to hold moisture in hands and nails and prevent their drying out. And be sure to use those rubber gloves with cotton lining.

Nail wrapping (pages 48– 49) strengthens nails but won't correct the problem, so continue to keep the nails as supple as possible. Evening primrose oil, vitamin B (pyridoxine), and vitamin C all have their supporters, but there is no scientific evidence that these treatments are effective. Frequent use of moisturizers and protection against chemicals *is* a good defense though.

Brittle nails can also result from a medical problem, such as severe vitamin A deficiency, calcium disease, or thyroid disease, but they will usually improve if the underlying cause is corrected. Patience may be required, since regardless of the cause and treatment you may have to wait six to eight months before a new nail plate has grown in.

Thin and weak nails often occur after a crash diet or during and following menopause, but some people are just born with this tendency.

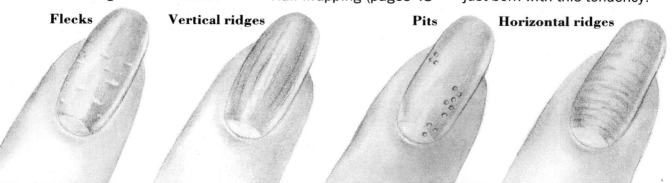

Flecks **Vertical ridges** **Pits** **Horizontal ridges**

Pitting (little round pits), crumbling, or nails that pull away from underlying skin is often associated with increasing age. It can also be caused by psoriasis, a chronic skin condition that can be treated by a dermatologist.

Transverse grooves, known as Beau's lines, are deeper than simple ridges. They usually begin near the cuticle, growing out as the nail grows. Grooves may be caused by too vigorous use of an orangewood stick, causing damage to the nail matrix, but also can be caused by internal stress and trauma, infectious diseases, pregnancy, heart disease, emotional shock, or alcoholism.

SPECIAL TIP: If your nails are brittle, try hot oil treatments, and avoid nail enamels for a while. Attractive results can be achieved from buffing. As the nails improve, you can follow a light buffing with a coat of nail polish.

MISSHAPEN NAILS

Some people have a natural tendency to spooning or bending upward of the nail, and this is nothing to worry about. Thin and concave nails can be caused by long-term use of strong soaps or sometimes from an illness.

Claw nails are somewhat unattractive but usually not serious. The nail may be thick and twist or curve inward; nails can also become clawlike from an injury.

Occasionally the shape of the nails itself may indicate underlying medical problems. For instance, a swollen and raised nail base can indicate heart or lung disease. Where there is prolonged oxygen deficency, fingertips can get thick and soft, and the nail can develop a true club shape. Club nails can also occur from repeated injury to the fingers.

Claw nail

Spoon nail

Hangnail

COMMON PROBLEMS

Hangnails are painful, but usually avoidable. Hangnails and inflamed cuticles involve a small painful tear or split in skin around the nail edges. Very dry skin or injury can cause it; nail biting or picking at nails are frequently the culprits. Excessive use of cuticle removers and nailbrushes, or careless cutting of the cuticle can exacerbate the problem. Carefully cut any hangnails with a pair of well-sanitized cuticle nippers or a pair of sharp-pointed manicure scissors, and apply an antiseptic to avoid infection. If hangnails—or any injury on or around the nails—are recurrent, painful, or become inflamed, infected, or if pus appears, see a physician, who may recommend a tetanus shot or antibiotics taken internally.

Many of the conditions I have described can initially be treated at home. If you have very sensitive skin, you may be allergic to some nail cosmetics and products, although this is less common than many people think. Actually, you are more likely to develop redness or a rash or itch behind the ear, on the eyelids, or some other sensitive spot that you have touched with still-damp polish or hardeners.

In the early 1970s the Food and Drug Administration (FDA) made a policy statement about formaldehyde saying that it could be safely used in concentrations not exceeding five percent, if the manufacturers and consumers followed certain guidelines. The FDA recommends that when you use products containing formaldehyde that you are careful to use them only on the tip of the nail, and that you use a nail shield to protect the skin. None of the major cosmetic companies have used formaldehyde in their nail products for many years, but dermatologists report that formaldehyde is beginning to creep back into some products, especially those made by small independent companies and sold in beauty supply shops and drug stores. Dermatologists recommend you look carefully at labels, as these products can lead to bacterial infections of the nail, inflammation of the nail folds, or cause the nail to separate from the nail bed. If you suspect a reaction to a product, stop using it and try a nonprescription cortisone cream. Follow directions carefully, and if you don't see rapid improvement, consult a dermatologist.

If you have a cut, separation of nail from base, or the beginning of an infection, use a good antiseptic, such as white iodine, over and under the nail and a non-prescription antibiotic ointment. Again, if it persists or worsens, see a physician.

The condition of nails is an important clue to disease and for this reason, if you ever undergo surgery you may be asked to remove colored polish so that your nails can be carefully monitored. At any time, major changes in your nails should be called to the attention of your family physician or a dermatologist. Many times the condition of nails may be an aid in diagnosis of skin disease elsewhere, or as a marker of internal disease. Some conditions are inherited or congenital; others are not.

A VISIT TO THE DERMATOLOGIST

See a dermatologist if you have pain, bleeding, pus or other discharge from the nail, or any other persistent nail problems such as those discussed earlier. Ask your family doctor for a recommendation, or call your local county medical society for the names of dermatologists in your area. You can also consult the directory of medical specialists (in most public libraries) for the names of board-certified dermatologists near you.

A dermatologist will examine your nails (remove polish before you go there) under a good light. He or she will be looking for conditions such as trauma or psoriasis, which may affect only one or all parts of the nail.

Before you visit, you may want to give some thought to the questions the doctor is likely to ask:

• When did this problem begin? Has it changed since it began?
• Have you ever had it before?
• Which nails were first affected?
• Were you born with this problem?
• Does anyone else in your family have the problem?

• What is your occupation?
• What are your hobbies?
• Do you play any musical instruments? (Guitar players are subject to nail injuries.)
• Have you ever had the following conditions or illnesses? (depending on your problem):

　　skin problems such as psoriasis, ringworm
　　yeast infections
　　cardiac or pulmonary conditions
　　allergies
　　autoimmune diseases such as lupus, scleroderma, forms of arthritis
　　diabetes
　　thyroid problems

• What kind of hand soap do you use?
• Do you use any strong soaps, hair straighteners, or dyes?
• What medications or drugs do you take internally?
• What medications or non-prescription items do you use on your skin?
• What brands of polish, base coat, top coat, hardeners, and cuticle treatment do you use?

• Do you recall hurting the nail?
• Do you pick at your nails, bite them, tear them off?
• Do you (or does a manicurist) push your cuticle back or cut it?

A dermatologist's careful history and examination should yield the cause of your problem and an appropriate treatment. But if the answer isn't obvious, the dermatologist may want to do some cultures and a biopsy of the nail itself.

Most of these nail problems are easily avoided by taking proper care of your hands. Even those conditions that seem chronic and persistent can be overcome. Those problems requiring medical attention are rarer; with a little care, hands and nails can be healthy all the time.

2 THE RIGHT EQUIPMENT

To achieve a professional salon manicure look you need the proper tools—not a lot of exotic gadgets, but a few high-quality items that you maintain carefully.

Much of what you need to keep your hands healthy and beautiful, and your nails strong and lovely, can be found right in your own bathroom and kitchen cabinets. You may also have a lot of unnecessary items that are of little value in achieving a good manicure. And you'll probably need to invest in a few supplies and implements before you can give yourself a complete, professional manicure at home.

WHAT YOU ALREADY HAVE

Before you march off to the nearest cosmetic counter, only to be coaxed into buying everything in sight, look around your home; you may already own many of the things you'll need.

IN THE KITCHEN You are likely to find an 8- to 10-ounce plastic bowl in the kitchen, perhaps left over from a take-out order. This will be perfect for soaking your fingers; you just need room to soak one hand at a time.

While you're there, add a coffee filter or a tea bag to your collection. Either one is fine for wrapping a nail in an emergency. Fill a small plastic bottle with dishwashing liquid; you will be using this to loosen dirt and soften cuticles when you soak your hands. You will need some oil to moisturize and prevent wet nails from smudging, so put aside some olive, sesame, mineral, or sunflower oil for these purposes.

HEAD FOR THE BATH-ROOM Your medicine cabinet contains some important supplies. Alcohol makes a fine disinfectant for cleaning tools and touching up a nick. Your man's styptic stick may come in handy if you get a little too aggressive pushing back your cuticle. Hydrogen peroxide can be used to whiten stained

nails (along with or instead of a lemon), and white iodine is a great disinfectant if you cut yourself or spot any early signs of bacterial infection under the nail.

Look for a roll of cotton or some cotton balls. Put some in a small plastic sandwich bag or a clean take-out container with a cover. Cotton-tipped swab sticks are great for removing polish smudges or mistakes. Put a number of them with your supplies.

SPECIAL TIP: Don't use synthetic cotton; the fibers can attach to your nail, leaving it bumpy. Use pure cotton instead.

You will want a pumice stone for smoothing off any dry skin, and a nice soft nail-brush or soft old toothbrush for gently cleansing the nails.

Did you come across that rusty old toenail clipper yet? Don't try to revive it. Any clippers or nippers that look like they have seen better days should be tossed out.

Look over your supply of hand and body lotion. You

should have enough so that you can put one bottle with your manicure supplies and strategically place the others in each bathroom, on your bedside table, in your desk drawer, kitchen, and even near the garden hose! Sample sizes are perfect for some of these places.

Finally, add a few vitamin E capsules from your vitamin supply.

IN THE BEDROOM Probably lying in your top dresser drawer in its original case is the leather manicure set your grandmother gave you for your sixteenth birthday. Most of what's in the kit isn't much use—the metal pusher for your cuticles can do damage, and the metal file is even worse. But the cuticle nippers may be just fine if they are still in excellent condition with a sharp and smooth jaw edge. And save that beautiful case for the new tools you will be buying.

WHAT YOU'LL NEED TO BUY

There is a huge array of nail products and equipment on the market today, and it is very tempting to go overboard when you see all of them lined up in the department store or pharmacy. Some of these products are really next to useless, and a few are downright harmful. Take the checklist on page 18 with you, and stick to it, avoiding temptations. (Naturally, if you found some of those items at home, you won't need to buy them.)

After you complete your shopping list, head for a large discount drug store or a professional beauty supplies dealer. (Or see the reference guide on page 86 so you can order by mail.) Read product ingredients, avoiding those with formaldehyde if you have ever been allergic or even sensitive to cosmetics. Shop in stores that have a big turnover, so that products don't exceed their three- to six-month shelf life.

And stay away from gimmicks! Don't even consider one of those dome-shaped nail driers or the electric filing, buffing, and scrubbing machine with its assortment of attachments. They are completely useless. Nail drying sprays don't speed up drying, and they can dull your polish as well.

CUTICLE NIPPERS This will be your only major investment. Choose one described as a ¼ or ½ jaw. Pick it up and squeeze it gently to see if the spring moves smoothly. A top-notch pair of nippers may cost you anywhere from $10 to $20.

ORANGEWOOD STICKS I prefer the thinnest ones, but any width will do. They usually come three to a box and you will find them indispensable for pushing back cuticles, cleaning under your nails, and for nail wrapping.

TOENAIL CLIPPERS This is a moderately priced item—only about a dollar or so. Get a large one with a straight edge for toenails, and a smaller one for trimming down extra-long fingernails.

EMERY BOARDS An essential part of your equipment. The familiar dark tan ones are fine for toenails, and if you have very long, extra-strong fingernails, you can use them for those nails, too. But for the average person, or one who is still working on nail growth, the dark tan ones are too coarse. One good swipe with this emery board can erase everything you have so tenderly and patiently nurtured. Instead buy emery boards that are of a fine-grade texture. I like the black ones (they're hard to find, but worth the search) for shaping, and then a blue or pink buffing disc or a smoothie (an emery board look-alike with a foam core, without the sandpaper) for smoothing away any rough edges. You will find these especially good during the early stages of nail growth.

SPECIAL TIP: If you do go to a salon for an occasional manicure, bring your own nippers, orangewood sticks, emery boards, and buffing discs. Few salons practice hospital-like sterilization methods so this is the *sure* way to avoid any possible contamination from a previous client who might have a transmissible disease.

NAIL POLISH REMOVER Get both a large bottle *and* a very small one to carry with you, in a scent that appeals to you. I recommend an oily nail polish remover if you're watching your budget, a non-acetone one if you're feeling a bit extravagant or if your nails tend to be dry or brittle. Don't buy pure acetone, thinking it will do a better job than nail polish remover. It won't and is just about guaranteed to dry out your nails.

You may have noticed remover in a dip-jar. I don't recommend this product for several reasons. The sponge absorbs old polish and can leave a residue of color on your fingers. It is also very drying to immerse the whole finger.

Individual sealed packets of remover on towelettes are handy, but they are costly to use. However, they are great for travel, or to tuck in your handbag or desk drawer for occasional use.

A polish corrector, which looks like a soft-tipped marking pen but is filled with nail polish remover, is a good addition to your supplies. It easily erases stray polish from around nails and cuticles.

NAIL ENAMELS Before buying, check out the polish already on your shelves. If it looks lumpy, a few drops of nail solvent or thinner may rescue it; if not, throw it out. And read chapter 4 to determine which shades are best for you.

Be particularly careful to buy polish that has not exceeded its shelf life. Give the bottle a good shake; if it just sits there looking thick and lazy, it may have already started down the road to obsolescence.

There is really no reason to buy expensive polishes; their formulations are seldom any better than the mass market ones, but they *may* offer a more interesting variety of colors. Some brands of polish are labeled "one coat." Try one if you wish; they are not all of high quality.

SPECIAL TIP: When buying nail polish, be sure that the handle on the brush is comfortable. And never buy more than one bottle of a new brand until you're convinced that you like the texture of the polish, and that the brush is of good quality and easy to grip.

CUTICLE SOFTENER
Do not confuse this with cuticle remover. Look at the bottle carefully so you don't come home with the wrong product.

CUTICLE OIL OR CREAM
These super-emollient products help keep the cuticles supple, preventing tears and hangnails. However, baby oil (or salad oil) works just as well for this purpose, so you needn't buy an expensive cuticle oil unless you prefer the consistency or the convenience of the small container.

LIQUID FIBER-WRAP BASE COAT
Everyone should own a bottle. It is great for peeling or weak nails and can even repair small breaks. It's a modestly priced item and I suggest that you use it weekly.

BASE COAT AND TOP COAT
Don't scrimp; buy a good brand, and if it does have formaldehyde (I prefer the ones that are formaldehyde-free for reasons of allergies and sensitivity) be sure that it contains less than five percent. The base coat's purpose is much like that of a primer applied to raw wood. It will enable polish to go on more smoothly, avoid staining the nails, keep the color truer, and make it more chip resistant. A ridge filler is especially good under light-colored polish because it is fairly opaque and even prevents streaks. A good nail strengthener can help prevent splitting, chipping, and peeling. I like to use a ridge filler as a base coat. This is an opaque white or beige tint that dries to a dull finish, filling in any ridges and preventing staining of the nail from dark-colored polishes. The top coat should be a long-wearing one with acrylic.

BUFFER AND BUFFING PASTE
There are times when you may want to go without polish and this will protect your nails as well as give them a finished look. And it's perfect for doing a man's manicure.

INSTANT NAIL GLUE
This fast-drying adhesive is used for all kinds of repairs, extensions, and nail-wrapping procedures. Its consistency makes it spread over the nail surface quickly, and it is strong enough to keep an acrylic tip or wrap in place for months with the proper upkeep. Be sure to buy a product specifically intended for use on the nails; the instant bonding household glues have a stronger formulation that is more harmful to skin and is more difficult to work with.

OVERNIGHT NAIL TIPS OR ACRYLIC NAIL TIPS
To lengthen your nails artificially, for a special occasion or semipermanently. You may also want a bottle of acrylic filler powder if you choose the acrylic tips. See chapter 6 for more on extensions and repairs.

NAIL-CARE CHECKLIST

Some of the manicure and pedicure supplies on this list may be optional, depending on your needs, but this is a comprehensive list and you will never need anything that isn't on it.

Equipment:
- finger bowl (8 to 10 ounces for soaking hands)
- large bucket, mixing bowl, or basin for pedicures

Implements
- orangewood sticks
- emery boards: dark tan, black
- smoothing discs or smoothies
- chamois nail buffer
- cuticle nippers
- toenail clippers
- rubber or strong plastic gloves with cotton liners
- surgical gloves
- cotton gloves
- nail brush (soft)
- pumice stone
- clean hand towel
- toe holder (a sponge-rubber device that separates the toes, preventing smudging while polishing)
- small pair of scissors (for cutting patches, small bandages, etc.)

Beautifiers
- cleansers, such as a liquid soap
- alcohol (for disinfecting tools)
- white iodine
- nail polish remover
- cuticle softener
- hydrogen peroxide
- hand creams or lotions
- sloughing agent
- instant nail glue
- cotton balls or roll
- cotton-tipped swabs
- styptic stick
- tissues
- buffing paste
- ridge filler base coat
- liquid fiber wrap
- top coat or nail strengthener
- selection of polishes
- quick-dry oil (or baby or salad oil)
- nail patch paper or filter paper
- nonprescription antibiotic cream or ointment
- Band-Aids
- Optional: solvent or thinner; silk or linen wraps; acetate tips; vitamin E capsules; nail polish corrector; cuticle cream or oil; nonprescription cuticle cream

STORING YOUR EQUIPMENT

Some women claim that the reason they don't do their own nails is that it's too much trouble to gather everything together. "By the time I have it all ready, I could have been back and forth to the salon" is a common excuse.

Others tell me that whenever they're in the middle of a manicure they discover they're missing something they need.

The solution—get everything organized! You'll need some kind of container: a small plastic drawer organizer, a wicker basket, or even a strong men's shoebox is fine. Clear plastic shoe or sweater storage boxes sold in housewares departments work well, and so do refrigerator and freezer containers. My favorite storage receptacle is a large, zippered, clear plastic toiletries bag.

SPECIAL TIP: Avoid direct light from an overhead incandescent lamp. They generate heat, which causes polish to bubble.

Whatever your choice, find a place to keep your container that is out of your way but handy to take out once a week. Make sure that everything is tightly closed to prevent spills and evaporation. And be sure that everything is away from children and pets. Nail polish remover in particular, especially if it contains acetone, is poisonous; so is nail glue. If someone should swallow any of these, call your local poison control center immediately. Remember, too, that when children are face-to-face with bright nail polish, they develop a remarkably creative urge to paint themselves and anything else around.

SPECIAL TIP: Keep nippers in a separate container so their tips won't dull.

Replace orangewood sticks when they get soiled or worn at the edges. Emery boards need frequent replacement, and buffing discs will eventually no longer do their job. Nail

---

PACKING A TRAVEL KIT

Think of this as an emergency kit or a "satellite station." You may want to keep one in your briefcase, in a tote you take away for weekend visits, or in your desk at the office. Keep everything in a small case with a zipper.

These items belong in your carrying case:

nail glue (place a straight pin in the hole so it doesn't leak)

emery board

buffing disc

small tube of hand cream

Band-Aids (in case your nail breaks below the skin line) and a pair of small scissors for trimming them

packet of nail polish remover

base coat

top coat

the nail polish you are currently wearing

---

brushes should be kept clean; rinse well after each use. They can also develop straggly bristles, which can catch on your cuticle and start a hangnail, so replace them when they are worn.

With these supplies in good order, you're all set to get your nails in shape!

MAINTENANCE

Good cooks keep their tools in good condition, and so do mechanics. If you care about your nails, please keep your tools and supplies in good order.

Your cuticle nippers—the biggest investment you will make in nail care—should be properly tended. Sanitize them with alcohol *before* and *after* each use, even if you are the only person using them. Sharpen them every six months, either by returning them to the manufacturer or at your local knife sharpener. Many local hardware stores offer that service; if not, look in your Yellow Pages under "Sharpening Service." Nippers should be kept well oiled; Put a drop of oil in the center screw weekly, and in the spring hinge when it begins to get a bit stubborn.

3 GETTING IN SHAPE

Some people instinctively know the correct shape for their nails, but most people, I have found, do not. There is an ideal nail shape and length for everyone, determined by finger size, nail-bed width, and life-style.

To achieve a well-balanced, graceful look, nails should be shaped like the fingertips. But that doesn't mean you are locked into this shape; you can adapt current styles to your individual growth pattern and shape, as well as your life-style. An active woman may be more comfortable with fairly short nails, even if her fingers are long and tapered. Although a soft square with rounded corners is most stylish today, women with short and wide fingers will look more feminine with an oval-shaped nail. Some tricks with color, which are described in chapter 5, can help nails look longer, thinner, or wider.

THE LONG AND SHORT OF IT

Fortunately the era of the Manchurian dragon lady nails is long since gone. At one time wealth and position were determined by the length of nails; a woman with servants and ample leisure time was able to grow her nails as long as she wanted. Today extra-long nails just look tacky. Everyone knows that *anyone* can simply glue on long nails. Well-groomed, well-proportioned nails attest to you as a fashion-conscious person who is meticulous but not obsessed with appearance.

Within the range of what is stylish and acceptable today, there are three basic nail lengths: short, average, and long.

Short length nails are those in which the free edge reaches only to the tip of the finger.

Average length nails are those in which the free edge extends about one-quarter of the length of the nail plate.

Long length nails are those in which the free edge extends beyond the fingertip from one-third to one-half the length of the nail plate.

Well-groomed short nails, contrary to common belief, can be polished with any color that is right for your coloring, clothes, and life-style. Average length nails are a reasonable goal for anyone who indulges in normal activities that may put nails at risk of breakage. That includes the woman who is careful not to use her nails as tools, but *does* have to do some everyday things such as bathing the kids, reaching into a pocketbook for keys, and filing papers.

Long nails are glamorous and provide an attractive backdrop for rings. But any-thing longer than one-half the nail bed is just *too* long. It looks ungainly, and will create unnatural pressure on the nail base, which can result in trauma to the nail and painful breaks below the free edge.

Short, average, and long lengths

THE BEST LENGTH

Here's a simple quiz that will help you determine the most becoming length for your nails:

- **Do your nails turn up (convex) or down (concave)?** Keep your nails short, or try artificial nail tips with new, flattering shapes (page 51).
- **Do you do a lot of gardening? Swimming? Handle ice-skates or ski buckles? Use an adding machine or calculator?** If so, avoid long nails, which are prone to breakage and can be awkward.
- **Are your hands small in proportion to your body size?** Longer nails will be flattering.
- **Are your hands large in proportion to your body size?** Keep nails average length.
- **Are your fingers thick, hands large?** Try nails slightly longer than average.

If your nails barely extend beyond the fingertip, you will need a little patience to develop average length nails. Be even more patient if you are dreaming about long nails. But that's fine, because even with care, it takes time to get used to using your hands with longer nails.

Remember, expect about one-eighth inch of nail growth a month. In about two months you should be able to go from short, clipped nails to average nails, or from average length to long nails. (You don't need to be a mathematician to recognize that the longer your natural nail bed, the longer it will take you to have long nails.)

THE SHAPE YOU'RE IN

Even more important to the appearance of your nails than their length is the shape in which you choose to file them. In general, nails look most natural if their shape subtly follows the shape of the nail base, whether it's round, square,

pointed, or oval (see illustration, page 25). But nails *can* be reshaped to disguise less than model-perfect hands or nails that are not well-proportioned for the hand. However you decide to shape your nails, avoid more than just a touch of filing on the sides of the nails. You need that side support, and if you file too much the nail will become extremely susceptible to breakage. The only exception is convex or concave nails.

Short stubby hands often have square nail beds, and these hands look best with oval nails. It's not too difficult to achieve this—when you file them, take just a very little off the side. This will help achieve the optical illusion of longer, thinner nails.

Nail shaping for short, stubby hands

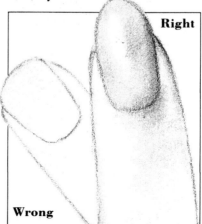

Right

Wrong

Nail shaping for nails with a round base

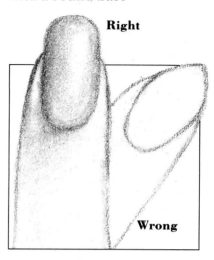

Right

Wrong

Nails with a round base look best if they are only slightly tapered, and the free edge extends just past the tip of the finger. They look good with a soft square on the top with slightly rounded edges. (This is sometimes referred to as an umbrella shape.)

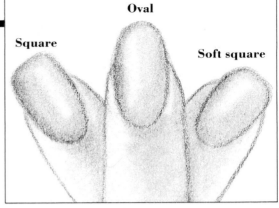
Shaping options for oval-based nails

If you have *oval nails* you are lucky; you can choose any shape you like. However, the oval look will be the most natural and attractive.

Narrow or lean nails can easily look like daggers if they are too tapered. Even oval nails can make you look like you're ready to claw someone rather than shake hands, if they aren't blunt and rounded. These nails look best with a soft square look.

SPECIAL TIP: As a matter of fashion and good taste, pointed nails look dreadful on everyone. Contrary to the opinion of some old-fashioned manicurists, pointed nails will *not* make stubby hands look more tapered, nor will they make short nails appear longer. And pointed nails *never* enhance the glamour of long fingers and nails.

Long, lean fingers

Nails that fan out as they leave the free edge are more common than many people think. Carefully file the sides straight and shape the top oval. This will make your nails look as if they had grown in an oval shape.

Concave or convex nails should be kept short, then shaped oval or rounded. Extending them, even slightly, beyond the free edge will only draw attention to the unusual shape. If your heart is set on long nails, clip your own nail very short and re-create a new shape with an artificial nail, as described in chapter 6.

Finger shapes vary among people and even from finger to finger. Everyone has a finger that seems to say, "How did I get into this family of nine look-alikes?" This isn't a crooked finger, but one that seems to curve or tilt a bit to one side. File this nail ever so slightly against the shape of the finger. This creates an optical illusion, making the finger appear to match the others.

Whether you have short, average, or long nails, if they are neatly shaped so that each finger seems to match the others, you will look feminine, attractive, and well-groomed.

Nail shaping

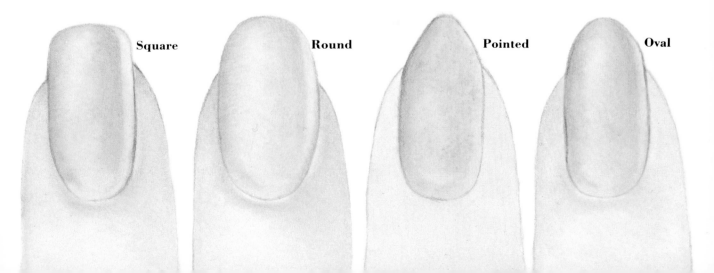

Square   Round   Pointed   Oval

IT'S A
COLORFUL
WORLD

4

The best thing about nail polish, or enamel, as it is often called, is that there are so many to choose from—*and* you can buy several bottles. You don't have to buy the most expensive polish, just don't economize on bases and top coats. Polish can last a long time if you invest in some solvent, and regardless of your coloring, you can choose from a number of shades.

If I could give my clients only one piece of advice about nail polish, it would be this: Don't limit yourself to one color. Change colors according to the time of the year, your mood, your current wardrobe, or your anticipated activities for the following week.

Many people believe that if they have short nails they are limited to the palest shades; or perhaps a French manicure. Nothing could be further from the truth. Short nails can look stunning and sophisticated impeccably polished bright red.

Color is becoming for all women even if it's just a hint. Nail enamel offers protection as well as beauty, and it's especially good for those who may have blemishes on their nails. And, when your nails look beautiful, you are more likely to treat them with care.

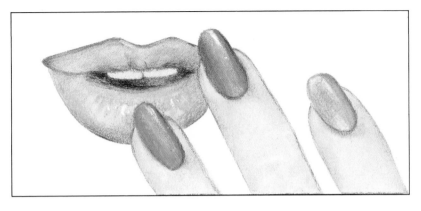

THE COLOR FOR YOU

You may already know which makeup shades are most flattering to your skin tone—the right color is absolutely de rigueur for your lips, but you can be more flexible in choosing nail colors.

If you don't already know your best colors, discuss color selection with a salesperson at the cosmetic counter of a large department store or drugstore. These salespeople have often been trained in color analysis, as have those in direct-sales of cosmetics at home and office. There are also many books available that address color. In many communities color consultants help fashion-conscious women find their palette. Within that family of colors there are a number of choices, and if you stay with those colors in clothes as

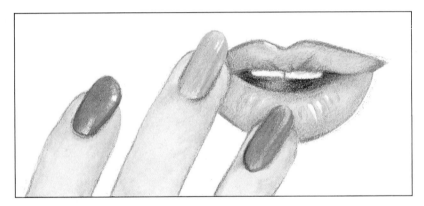

Top to bottom:
Best shades for 1) pink/blue, rosy beige or brown-toned skin; 2) ivory, peach or golden skin; 3) pale, olive or black skin

well as makeup you will find that the polish you are wearing today is not likely to clash with the clothes you wear tomorrow.

Following is a primer on choosing colors—and remember that while your lips, fingernails, toenails, shoes, pocketbook, and sweater don't have to match, they shouldn't fight with each other, either.

If you have pinkish blue or rosy beige or brown undertones to your skin, you probably look best in pink or burgundy lipsticks, blushes, and polishes. But you will also look great in watermelon reds, mauvey pinks, and coral browns. Your wardrobe contains many different colors, but generally you will stay away from the olives, golds, and oranges.

Those with ivory, peach, or golden brown skin can usually wear warm colors such as oranges, rusts, and dark tomato reds. They look good in lipsticks and nail polishes with these undertones. But that doesn't mean they can't wear light polishes; peachy pinks work beautifully.

WEEKEND MAKEOVER

Although you shouldn't remove polish more than once every five to seven days (remember, remover is drying), you can still have a brighter or more exciting look on the weekend than during the week. Give yourself a manicure on Sunday night (or Monday morning if you're one of those people who likes to watch the sun rise) using a pale color suitable for work. Then on Friday, simply put a top coat of dark or bright polish over it. Finish with a clear top coat. Presto: a fresh-looking manicure with a glamorous weekend color. Sunday or Monday, start all over again with a complete manicure and your weekday color choice.

Peachy or golden brown–skinned people tend to look good in many bright colors as well, including bright and orange reds, corals, and peach. Nail polishes can have the same tones.

Those with very pale, olive, or black skin look great dressed in black, dark greens, blues, magenta, and many shades of red. Nail polishes in icy pink, deep pink, and blue and true reds are flattering.

Even within these ideal color ranges, there are variations. Summertime calls for paler colors than fall or winter so if you love the pale pinks in July, change to mauve in September. When the leaves turn on the trees, go from watermelon or jelly apple reds to deep berries, peach to a clear bright red, and bubble gum pink to a deeper magenta.

VARIETY IS THE SPICE OF LIFE

In the days when I worked in a private salon, I noticed that the middle-age and more mature women tended to suffer from a disease I call "RC," resistance to change. Many of those women would find a flattering color and then stay with it—week after week, month after month. It was tough trying to convince some of them that there is a beautiful spectrum of colors out there, and that it was a shame to limit themselves to only a few. But once they did begin to experiment, they were delighted to discover a new range of attractive colors.

Teens, on the other hand, often go to the other extreme, choosing blues, greens, and other eye-catching but unflattering colors. They often fall prey to the advertising hype and variety store displays that suggest that black iridescent polish, stripes, and decals will make their nails look beautiful. The temptations are so great that many young women change their polish as often as they change their clothes, not realizing that the constant use of nail polish remover dries out nails to the breaking point. When I have occasion to demonstrate nail care to groups of teens, I suggest that they look carefully at some of the sheer polishes with a hint of color, especially those with a very pale, translucent beige.

GOOD FOR EVERYONE: THE FRENCH MANICURE

A good look for young or old is the French manicure. Sometimes called the California look, this seems to flatter everyone, regardless of the nail length. It's a little difficult to do at first, but easily mastered with practice. A step-by-step description is on page 44.

The French manicure, usually thought of as a sheer nude or beige polish applied over a whitened free edge, has many variations. You can polish the tip ivory instead of white; and instead of a beige top coat try any number of pinks, from light to frosty, or even a peach or apricot.

This look is ideal because it can take you from the boardroom to a late-night dinner party or country weekend. It looks as good with a gray or navy suit or formal dress as it will with sweats or jeans. I often give myself a French manicure when I go out of town on a demonstration or speaking tour because when I'm packing many different outfits I don't want to worry about taking the time to change my polish color.

COLOR FOR TOES

Years ago everyone said that fingers and toes should match just as they said shoes and bags should match. Today that seems a little passé and rigid. But you won't want to use an orange color on your toes and a pink on your fingers. Here's a simple rule: Don't match and don't clash. You can choose a clear deep red for your toes (polish usually lasts a few weeks on toes with only an occasional repair) and then you will be able to experiment with different shades of red for your hands.

Pale pinks can be used on your feet, but darker, brighter colors are more exciting and contrast much better with every sandal color.

FASHION SHOULDN'T DICTATE

Some of the most popular nail polish colors have been around for decades and will never go out of style. Others are a bit trendy, and come and go in a year or two. Don't let fashion dictate. Choose colors that flatter you and compliment the shades of your makeup and clothes.

And try different colors. Keep a bottle of solvent handy so you don't feel extravagant if you don't use up a color before you buy another, fearing it will get lumpy and be useless.

Look over your wardrobe and get a sense of the palette you have been wearing. Then check out the polish you have and head for your nearest cosmetic counter to choose a few new colors. It will provide you with more inspiration for giving yourself a lovely fresh manicure.

READY, 5 SET, POLISH

If you have always thought that you were inept at doing your nails, it's probably because you have been polishing them on the bus ride to the office or at night on the edge of your bed. If your polish always smears, is it because you have been too impatient to let it dry completely? Most disasters occur as a result of rushing.

A total of forty-five minutes a week is all you need to allocate from your busy schedule to have great-looking nails. And even that forty-five minutes isn't strictly "down time." You can listen to the radio or a tape (this is a good time to catch up on some taped books or how-to audios), watch television or talk on the phone. You can even read a book, if you turn the pages carefully.

Anytime you would like to give yourself a manicure is the right time. Just be sure to allot uninterrupted time. Early evening is good, because you are less likely to be tempted to start doing things before your nails are dry.

SPECIAL TIP: For a little extra moisturizing treatment, remove your polish the night before a manicure, put some petroleum jelly on your nails and cuticles, or better yet, pop open a vitamin E capsule and rub it in. Put on your white cotton gloves and let the moisturizing treatment do its magic overnight.

Remember to use a strong, clean, firm surface near a good light. Don't pull over a gooseneck lamp, allowing it to beam down its heat as well as light or, worse yet, do your nails at the beach or on the terrace. The sun will make the polish bubble. Spread a clean, thirsty towel you reserve for this purpose on the table. Remove all your implements

AFFORDABLE LUXURIES: HENNA AND LACTOL MANICURES

Salons charge almost double for these moisturizing treatments, but it will only cost you a few more pennies to treat yourself at home, and will take only a few extra minutes.

Henna is particularly good if you have been swimming in a chlorinated pool or spending too much time at pottery class, and your nails are beginning to show it. A henna manicure will bring back their pink glow, while at the same time adding an extra dose of moisturizer.

While preparing your supplies, combine two tablespoons of neutral (no color) pure henna and a half-cup of boiling water in the little bowl you have earmarked for soaking. Mix thoroughly, then add two tablespoons of mineral oil. Mix again. By the time you have filed your nails it will be comfortably warm.

A lactol manicure, called a European manicure in many salons, is one of the least expensive and most sinful luxuries in the world. It is a wonderful moisturizer and is especially good in the winter when nails are likely to become dry, and may even begin to curl upward. Lactol is a rich pink cream sold in beauty supply stores. You can, if you wish, buy a special heater for it, but it's not necessary; just put the lactol in a double boiler until it's warm or heat in the microwave or on an electric trivet.

and beautifiers from their storage container so you don't have to reach into it midway through the course of your manicure.

Next, fill your bowl with very hot soapy water—it will be just right by the time you get to it. Or, instead of soapy water, try a henna or lactol manicure.

Next, if the day is humid, or you are going to be in a hurry to dry your nails, fill another bowl with ice-cubes and just a bit of water. Take your phone off the hook or turn your answering machine on so you won't be interrupted. Turn the radio or television to the station you want, or open a book if you plan to read while your nails are drying.

A STEP-BY-STEP PROFESSIONAL MANICURE

STEP 1: REMOVE OLD POLISH

Take small pieces of cotton and roll them around in the palms of your hands. This helps remove most of those flyaway fuzzies, at the same time forming small balls. Then dampen one at a time with nail polish remover. In removing polish, as with all the following instructions, you should always start with the little finger of your dominant hand. Press the damp cotton over the nail for a few moments. You will feel the cotton start to slip when the polish begins to soften. Use a clean area of the cotton ball to remove the polish, wiping with a firm movement from the base of the nail to the tip. Don't rub back and forth; this will just inbed the polish into your cuticle. Continue, changing cotton as needed, until nails are completely clean.

If any polish stubbornly clings on or around the cuticle, roll a bit of cotton on the tip of an orangewood stick and dip into the remover to remove it.

If your nails are stained, gently buff the surface of your nail with a buffing disc in one direction to help remove stains, and rub a fresh lemon across nails.

STEP 2: SHAPE THE NAILS

Refer back to chapter 3 to decide on the nail shape best suited to your look and life-style. Be sure your nails are dry and have not just been soaking in the tub or dishpan, because they tear easily when softened by water. If your nails are very long, cut them with a nail clipper—*almost* but not completely to the desired length. Don't clip straight across in one movement; instead clip each side, then the center, approximating the shape you desire.

SPECIAL TIP: Very weak nails need your gentlest, undivided attention. Filing them before removing polish minimizes the chance of damaging them.

Next, with your fine-grain emery board held between the thumb and index finger at a 45-degree angle to your nail, gently begin to file in *one direction only,* taking two short strokes, and one long sweeping one. Don't saw back and forth; instead, work from each corner to the center of the nail. Gentle filing is imperative, because one disastrous swipe can eliminate your shaping options, leaving you nothing with which to work. Continue until you have the desired shape, avoiding the fragile corners, which can weaken the nails and create tears and splits. If you should get a tear in your nail, you will be able to repair it (as explained in chapter 6), but if you have filed away the corners you may have to cut the entire nail.

Once you have achieved the shape you want, smooth away any rough edges with your buffing disc, then check to see that the nails are smoothly filed, viewing them from two different angles. First hold your hand up and away from you, then curl your fingers into your palm. If the nails look even from both positions, you are ready to go on to the next step.

SPECIAL TIP: To be sure your nails are filed smoothly, run them across an old pair of hose. If the hose snag, go back to the buffing disc.

Applying cuticle softener

STEP 3: SOFTENING AND NEATENING THE CUTICLE

Apply cuticle softener all around the cuticles, then soak your right hand (left, if that's your dominant one) in the bowl of either warm soapy water, henna, lactol, or oil mixture. Leave your hand in the water for at least five minutes (ten minutes for lactol or oil). The cuticle softener and the soak will

Filing the nail

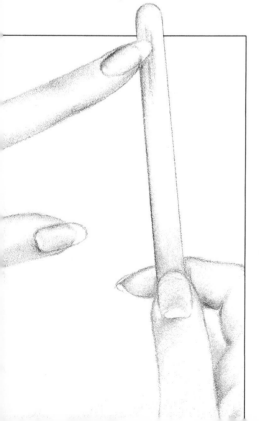

work together to loosen the cuticle. If your nails, fingers, and cuticles are imbedded with dirt from carbon paper or gardening, give them a good scrub with your soft brush.

Now, remove your hand from the water or oil, and gently push back your cuticles with the flat end of your orangewood stick. Be careful not to scratch the nail plate (another reason for not using an abrasive metal pusher), and use mild pressure to avoid injuring the root of the nail. Use the stick to clean under the nail.

With your well-sanitized cuticle nippers cradled in the upturned palm of your hand and the cutting edges on the underside, trim any hangnails. Use a light snip-and-pull, snip-and-pull motion. Do not cut the cuticle itself or attempt to remove it. You need some cuticle for protection against bacteria, and, if *that* doesn't convince you, remember that many experts believe that cutting will simply make it grow back faster.

If you nick yourself, don't panic! It's seldom anything more serious than a paper cut, and easily taken care of with a styptic stick or a cotton swab dipped in alcohol or peroxide.

Dry your hand; soak the other, and proceed again through Step 3.

SPECIAL TIP: If your nail tips are yellow, wrap some cotton on the orangewood stick and apply hydrogen peroxide to their undersides.

Trimming hangnails

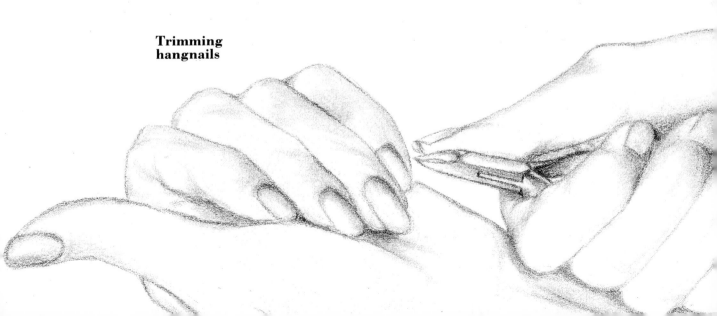

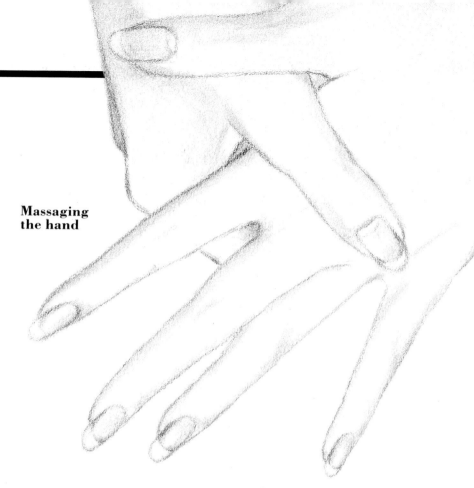

**Massaging
the hand**

STEP 4: MASSAGE HANDS AND FINGERS

Massage can relax the hand and encourage circulation to the nail root, resulting in better growth.

• Begin by bending each hand slowly with a forward and backward movement several times, resting your elbow on the table. This helps to limber the wrist.

• Next, place a dab of your favorite hand lotion or cream on the palm of one hand. With the other hand spread it over the hand, wrist, and fingers. Do not completely rub it in. Again, support your elbow on the table. With the cushions of the thumb of your other hand, apply some pressure and massage fingers in a circular motion. Continue downward to the

SPECIAL TIP: If your hands are extremely chapped, massage them with petroleum jelly or mineral oil instead of hand cream for extra-strength moisturizing, and allow it to soak in for 5 or 10 minutes.

wrist. Now, retrace your steps going backward to the starting position. Add additional dabs of lotion as hands become dry.

- Still resting your elbow on the table, hold each finger at the base, between the thumb and forefinger of the other hand, and rotate the finger several times.
- Encircle your wrist between the thumb and fingers of your other hand, gently rotating it three times.
- Open your hand as wide as possible, spreading your fingers. Then close to a tight fist. Repeat three times.
- Repeat with other hand.

STEP 5: CLEANUP

Rinse your nails well in the sudsy water, making sure to remove any cream residue with a wet cotton swab. Wrap an orangewood stick with a small amount of cotton to clean any cream from under the nails.

STEP 6: REPAIR DAMAGED NAILS

If you have a split or broken nail, follow the procedure outlined in chapter 6 before returning to Step 7. This is also the time to apply any wraps or extensions.

STEP 7: BUFFING

If you prefer to buff your nails instead of polishing them, (or top buffed nails with a single coat of clear polish) this is the way to do it. (Otherwise, proceed to Step 8.)

With your fingertip, apply a small dab of paste polish to each nail. Buff the nails with a buffer, stroking from base to nail edge or side to side. Lift the chamois buffer with each stroke to avoid a burning sensation. Continue until nails have a smooth, glossy appearance.

Buffing the nails

STEP 8: GETTING READY TO POLISH

Before polishing your nails, dip your cuticle nippers into alcohol or other disinfectant, dry carefully, and put them safely away. Discard used cotton, old emery board, soapy water or oil, and put away anything else you won't need.

Make sure that your base coat(s), polish, and top coat are lined up in front of you. Loosen the top on the top coat so you don't have to struggle with it after you have applied polish. If you must make a phone call, flip your album, or grab a cup of coffee, this is the time, because from now until your nails are dry, you should not do anything that could smudge them.

SPECIAL TIP: Place an orangewood stick in remover, in the event you need it to clean up any polish that spreads beyond your nail.

STEP 9: APPLY BASE COAT

If you have very short or problem nails, begin by applying a liquid fiber wrap. This product comes in a bottle with a brush, and is similar to other nail hardeners but it contains tiny fibers. It is far more effective than ordinary hardeners in treating peeling nails, very small tears or nails that are weak or fragile. Liquid fiber wraps are also excellent for first-time growers.

Apply one coat horizontally, allow to dry for a minute or two, then apply another coat vertically. This forms a weave effect, adding strength to your nails. Dry for five minutes.

SPECIAL TIP: Apply liquid fiber wrap—you will see significant results in six to eight weeks. Some companies recommend that you apply four coats of liquid fiber wrap. *Don't!* It will be much too thick and will take too long to dry.

Problem growers should next apply a ridge filler before proceeding with polish.

If your nails are problem free, you can omit the fiber wrap. Instead, use a formaldehyde-free nail hardener or strengthener, or a ridge filler. Remember: nail hardeners with formaldehyde should *only* be applied at the tips, avoiding contact with skin or cuticles.

Begin with your dominant hand, applying the product to your pinky first and working toward the thumb. Wait until dry before applying nail polish.

STEP 10: POLISH

Shake the polish vigorously, allowing a few seconds for bubbles to burst and settle. As you remove the brush, wipe the upper side of it against the inside of the neck of the bottle, allowing the excess polish to drip back into the bottle. If there's too much polish on the brush it will bleed into the cuticle.

Again, starting with the little finger of your dominant hand, paint the tips with a few quick strokes. This puts an extra coat of polish where you want it most. Then, using three sweeping strokes, apply a thin coat of polish lightly and quickly from base to free edge, first down the center, then down each side.

If any polish leaks into the cuticle, wipe away excess with the orangewood stick that you left standing in the bottle of remover.

Allow nails to dry for two minutes, then apply another coat. Two coats should be sufficient, but some light shades require a third coat to get a true color. Wait at least two minutes between each coat.

If you are using a very sheer color, apply 3 coats of color to get a truer reading of the color. Don't, however, apply your topcoat until the next day, as it will take too long for the additional layers of polish to dry. Proceed directly to Step 12.

If you have used a liquid wrap and a ridge filler, limit your polish to one coat, to avoid too much buildup.

Allow five minutes drying time before putting on a top coat or sealer.

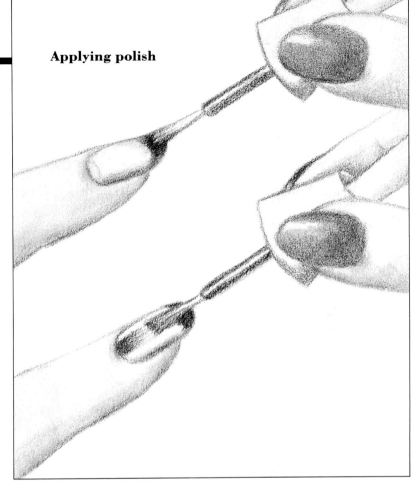

Applying polish

TROMPE L'OEIL POLISH

Generally speaking, nails should be shaped like the fingertips (see chapter 3 for more on shaping nails). But there are ways to alter the appearance of the nail's shape with nail polish.

• If you have naturally oval-shaped nails and long, thin fingers, you have several choices: you can keep the nails moderately long, and cover the entire nail with polish or, if you prefer shorter nails, you can leave a free edge *or* the half moon (lunula) at the base of the nail unpolished. This will give the nail a wider appearance.

wide nails | **or short, rounded nails**

• Short or very rounded nails will look longer if you leave a narrow margin on each side of the nail unpolished.

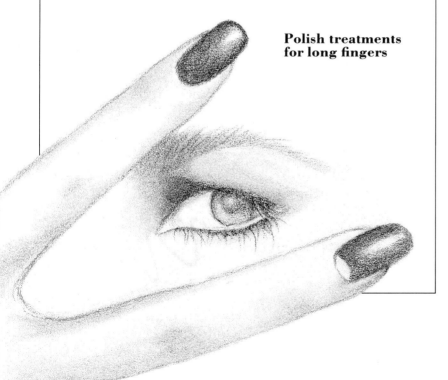

Polish treatments for long fingers

STEP 11: TOP COAT
A good top coat can extend the life of your manicure and give it a glossy "wet look" that is more finished. In addition, it helps prevent chipping. Many companies

SPECIAL TIP: If your polished nails bubble, it may be that you haven't been applying thin coats, have been using stale polish (when it thickens, use solvent, or toss it away and buy fresh polish), forgetting to let air bubbles rise and burst after shaking, or left some cream or oil on your nails. Sitting in front of an air-conditioner, fan, or bathroom heater will also make polish bubble.

SPECIAL TIP: If, despite your best behavior, you smudge a nail before it is dry, try this: Hold the thumb of your other hand tightly over the mouth of your nail polish remover bottle and carefully invert it so your thumb becomes wet with remover. Then gently rub your wet thumb over the smudge. Do this once or twice until the smudge is smooth. Then apply fresh polish.

make top coats, but clear polish will work just as well. Be sure it isn't thick. Apply top coat just as you do polish. If your nails are in very poor condition, use two coats of a strong nail hardener as a top coat.

STEP 12: OPTIONAL QUICK-DRY

If you are in a big hurry, or if the day is extremely humid, plunge your hands into the bowl of ice-water you prepared before beginning your manicure. This will help set the polish and speed up drying. Do it twice; once after the last coat of polish, and then again after the top coat. Putting your hands in front of a heater, or using a hair dryer, is almost guaranteed to cause bubbling and will *not* speed up drying. Since polish is inflammable, it's also a bit risky.

STEP 13: OIL FINISH

After your nails have had ten minutes to dry, apply baby oil or salad oil on and around your nails, using a good paint or cosmetic brush. This is an excellent drying aid, helping to set polish and avoid smudges. Some companies package quick-dry oil in a bottle with its own brush; this is very

useful and convenient. But *don't* use the canned aerosol quick-dries; they dull the polish.

On damp days, complete drying may take slightly longer, but generally you should be able to resume normal activities in a half hour. Give yourself a little extra time before digging into your pocketbook or filing cabinet and allow at least one hour drying time before you go to sleep, to avoid getting quilted smudges on your nails.

FRENCH MANICURE

The French manicure is really easier to do than most people imagine; just follow these simple directions:

1. Follow the steps for a basic manicure, up through the application of base coat (Step 9).

2. Next, using a #2 or #3 watercolor brush with a fine point, or an eyeliner brush, dip the brush in white, ivory, beige, or pale pink polish. Carefully following the natural line of the filed free edge, apply polish to the edge *only*. Allow three minutes for complete drying time.

3. Apply a coat of sheer nude beige, sheer pink, or any other pale, transparent color over the entire nail. Allow at least five minutes to dry.

4. Add another coat of sheer polish. Allow five minutes to dry.

5. Complete your manicure as usual, with top coat and quick-dry oil, if desired (Steps 11–13).

A new product on the market consists of narrow white and ivory oval-shaped adhesive strips that can be applied to the tips of the nails instead of painting them. The sheer polish is then applied over it as in the French manicure described above.

KEEPING YOUR MANICURE FRESH

To keep your manicure looking fresh all week apply one thin coat of clear polish or top coat every other day, followed with an oil finish. Allow to dry for ten to fifteen minutes.

If a nail chips, don't remove the polish. Simply buff the chip smooth with your buffing disc, then paint the chip with just a touch or two of polish. Allow to dry for five minutes, then apply one coat of a clear top coat.

If the polish is badly chipped or smudged, you will have to start all over again on that nail. Put a protective glove on your other hand. (Use a thick rubber one because the remover will eat through those lightweight surgical ones.) When you

THE FIVE-MINUTE MANICURE

That unexpected call for a job interview, dinner with the boss (yours or his), or from Mr. Right, always seems to happen when your nails are chipped. The solution: The five minute manicure. While not recommended as a weekly routine, it is extremely useful when time is of the essence. Before beginning, turn on your answering machine, get dressed, have your coat and pocketbook ready. Then follow these easy steps:

1. Remove old polish.
2. Smooth any rough edges with buffer (no time to reshape).
3. At sink, wash hands with soapy water. With orangewood stick, clean under nails and give a gentle push back on cuticles.
4. Rinse and dry hands thoroughly.
5. Apply one coat of pink- or beige-tone ridge filler. Allow to dry.
6. Apply one thin, clear top coat. Wait 2 minutes.
7. Apply quick-dry oil.

complete the "finger manicure" you may notice that the color looks a little darker than the other fingers. Don't worry; polish tends to oxidize quickly.

Whether you have given yourself the full treatment, or the five-minute manicure, your nails should look lovely. Remember to keep them looking fresh all week. If you should have a midweek disaster that demands immediate attention, you will find everything you need to know about repairs in the next chapter. If your heart is set on instant long nails, if you have seriously damaged nails, or you are a first-time grower, there is an answer to your cry of distress.

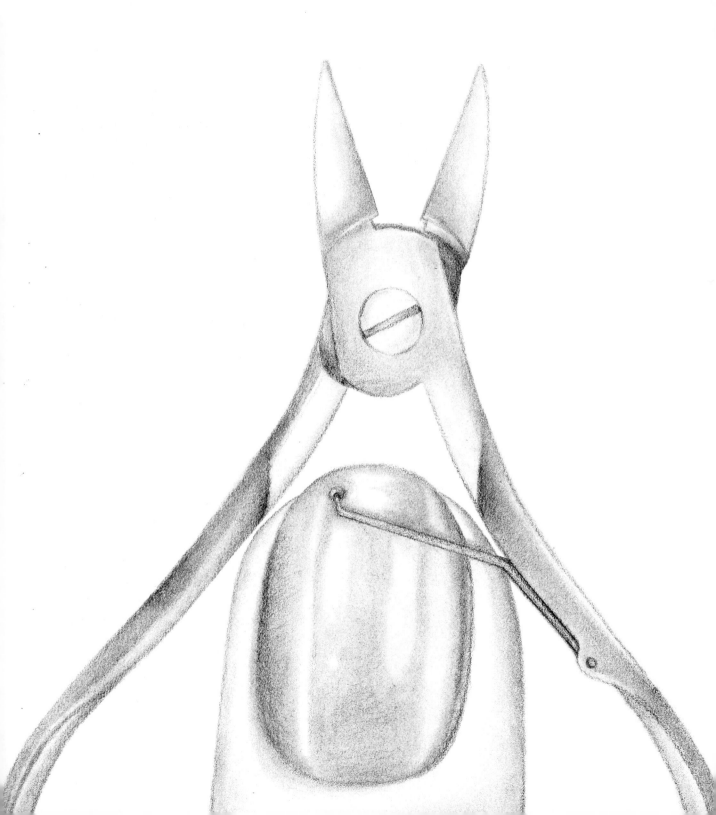

6 REPAIRS, STRENGTHENERS, AND EXTENSIONS

There's nothing more disheartening than a hand with four beautiful nails and one broken one. But you needn't despair, because repairs and extensions are not nearly as complicated as they sound. Most women—except those blessed with incredibly strong nails—can benefit from some extra help to strengthen, repair, or rebuild nails. And if your nails break easily or if you haven't broken the biting habit, there are a number of ways to solve your problem. With a little practice, you will be able to master most of these techniques.

REPAIRING A BROKEN NAIL

When you break a nail, you have a number of alternatives, from a quick fix to a wrap to a nail extension. If the nail breaks when you're at the office, an emergency (albeit temporary) repair will get you off to your next appointment looking your usual confident self (see box, next page). For more lasting results, or to add strength to weak or brittle nails, a wrap is your best choice.

NAIL WRAPPING

Silk, linen, cotton, paper, and cellophane can all be used to wrap nails that are weak, split, torn, or broken. These materials are glued onto the nails with the same instant nail glue described above. Solid wraps offer far more protection than the liquid fiber wraps described in chapter 5, and are really quite different. They are available in precut swatches, sometimes described as patches. You can use an old silk or cotton handkerchief or buy some sheer cotton batiste at a fabric store, or improvise, using a coffee filter, tea bag, or cellophane.

I prefer silk and cotton batiste; they are good for reinforcing nails of any length and for mending breaks. Linen is very good for extremely thick and brittle nails but its weight makes it very difficult to use, so leave linen wraps to the pros.

To wrap one nail or ten, follow the steps below, beginning with a naked nail. Complete one hand before proceeding to the other, if doing a complete wrap.

1. With buffing disc, buff the entire top of the nail lightly until it is smooth.

2. Apply nail glue corner-to-corner, from the free edge about one-third of the way down each nail, using the tip to spread the glue evenly. Follow the directions that come with the glue, being careful to use it sparingly, avoiding skin and cuticles.

3. Before this fast-drying glue has a chance to set, apply a piece of wrap to the tip of each nail. Let the material extend a bit over the free edge for now. It should *not* go under the nail. Hold wrap securely in place, so it doesn't slide, adjusting placement, if necessary, with an orangewood stick.

4. Apply more glue to the top of each nail wrap for additional reinforcement; the wrap material covering the nail should be completely saturated.

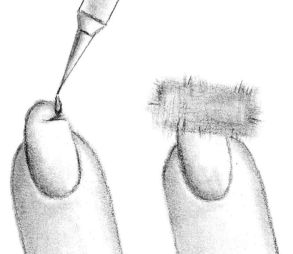
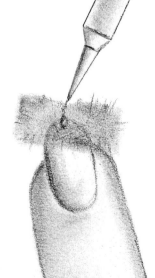

5. Wait a few seconds until it dries. You will note that the wrapping material has now hardened from the glue.

6. File excess wrapping material from the free edge and the sides of the nails, using your black emery board.

7. With a buffing disc, gently buff the surface of the wrap until it is flush with the nail, so you cannot see a line of demarcation. Fabric should look and feel smooth.

8. Apply a drop or two of glue to the top of each nail wrap. Allow it to dry.

9. With buffing disc, again buff the nail wrap until it is flush with natural nail.

10. Apply ridge filler base coat, nail color, and top coat, as described in chapter 5.

To change or remove polish from a wrapped nail, use a nonacetone remover; it won't loosen the glue. If you are caught short with only conventional remover, apply it as quickly and lightly as possible.

When you do your weekly manicure, or any time you change polish, proceed as usual, checking carefully to be sure wrap has not loosened, especially in corners. Apply a few drops of glue under *and* over loose areas, buff, and reapply polish.

The wrap should last until your nail has grown out, but if you should decide to eliminate the wrap, first remove the polish from the nail, then buff off the wrap with a buffing disc until you reach the natural nail. If you prefer, you can use a solvent manufactured for this purpose, but I find it tends to further dry the nails. Whichever method you choose, soak the nail in olive oil after removing the wrap to aid in restoring suppleness. If the nail seems soft or weak, apply two coats of liquid fiber wrap before applying base coat and polish.

SPECIAL TIP: If you want to use clear polish, be sure to wrap with silk; its sheerness avoids telltale evidence.

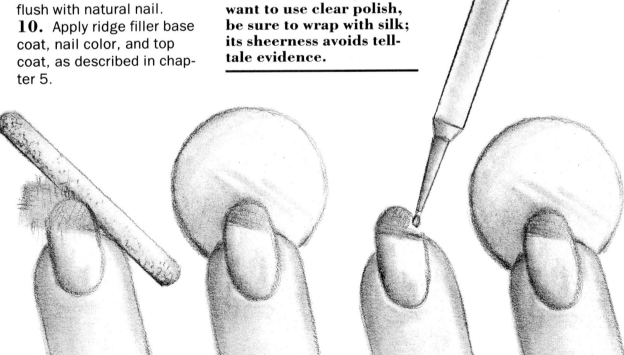

EMERGENCY NAIL REPAIR

For a quick fixit, follow this procedure:

1. Reach into your carrying case for remover and instant nail glue. (These liquidlike glues are very strong and dry in just seconds.)

2. Remove the polish from the broken nail.

3. Apply one drop of nail glue to the break. Be careful not to get it on your skin (it is irritating and can temporarily bond skin) or to use too much. If you do use more than you need it will delay drying time, but there is no need to wipe away excess.

4. Press the glued parts together and hold for a few seconds, until bond is set.

5. Allow to dry (five to ten seconds).

6. Add one more drop of glue.

7. Allow it to dry.

8. Apply a small piece of transparent tape to the break.

9. File away excess.

10. Buff smooth with buffing disc.

11. Apply base coat and polish.

12. Wait a minute or two to dry.

That evening do a more permanent repair, using either a wrap or an artificial nail tip.

SPECIAL TIP: Don't reapply part of a nail that has broken off. Once the nail is no longer attached it dries out and curls. Instead, use an artificial nail tip as a replacement.

Emergency nail repair

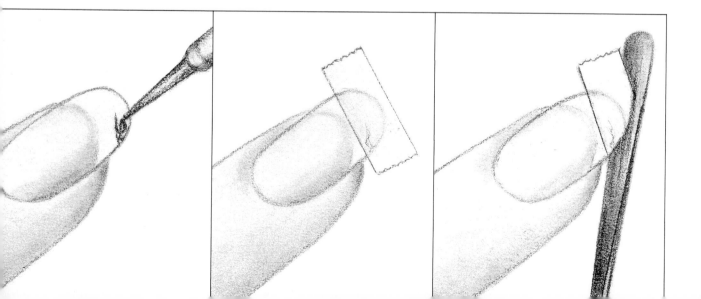

ARTIFICIAL AND ADD-ON NAILS

If you want to conceal broken or damaged nails, to offer protection to your own nails, to change their shape, or if you would like "instant" or temporarily beautiful nails for a special occasion, or to overcome nail-biting, nail tips and extensions can do the trick. Some can be done at home, others are best done by a professional.

You will find a wide variety of products at most drugstores and variety cosmetic counters, ranging from a number of easy-to-apply artificial and add-on nails (sometimes referred to as overnights) to more sophisticated products that are more lasting.

You can achieve a professional manicure at home with acetate tips that are affixed to your own nails, then covered with silk or acrylic. Sculptured (also known as acrylic or artificial) and gel nails are also used to lengthen short nails or replace broken ones; these are sometimes referred to as permanent. However, they do require regular maintenance and removal. Sculptured nails can look natural and beautiful and if placed carefully and hygienically and inspected regularly, they should not harm your own nails. These are either "built" onto acetate tips or onto a form that is temporarily placed under the tip of your own nail. Gel is applied to the nail (with or without an extension), and then your nails are placed under a "curing" light. They are then referred to as *bonded* nails. For best results, sculptured and bonded nails should be done by a professional.

Following is a fuller description of the various types of extensions, add-ons, and procedures.

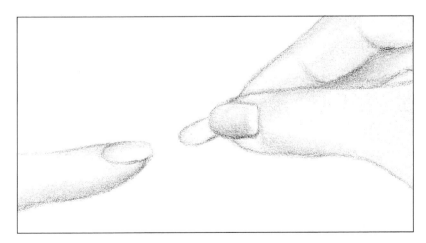

OVERNIGHTS These are artificial nails and the easiest ones to apply. They are available either colorless or already "polished." Some even have white tips to aid in creating a French manicure. They usually come with double-faced adhesive tabs with which to attach them to your own nails. Although these nails are not intended to remain on your nails for any length of time, they *are* meant to look good and last through an evening. Unfortunately, this isn't always the case.

These temporary nails tend to look unnatural because they seldom match the shape of your own nails or nail bed. And I have heard horror stories about nails that popped off at most unpropitious moments. But there are ways to use these clever nails for short periods so that they look more natural and stay where they belong.

Look carefully at the nails after you take them out of their package. Is the base the same shape as yours? If it's too wide or too square, simply file it with your black emery board, contouring each one individually to the exact shape of your nail bed (it may differ from finger to finger). This will give you a true-to-life fit. If the nails you have purchased are too long (it *is* possible to purchase them in "natural" or "active" lengths), trim them with clippers and then file them to achieve a natural look. They should not extend beyond the free edge by more than one-quarter to one-third of the length of the nail bed. This length will permit you to use your hands actively and the nails are far less likely to fall off.

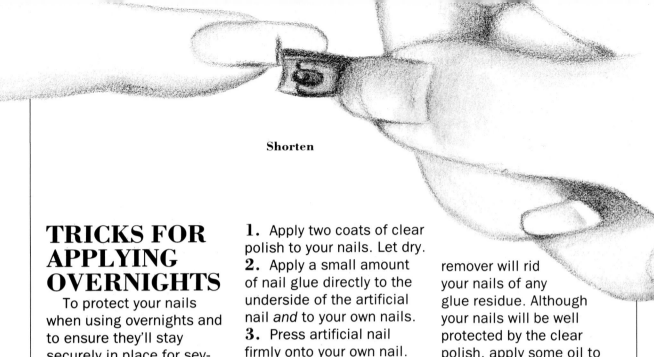

Shorten

TRICKS FOR APPLYING OVERNIGHTS

To protect your nails when using overnights and to ensure they'll stay securely in place for several hours, put aside the tabs that come with the nails and follow these instructions:

Glue

1. Apply two coats of clear polish to your nails. Let dry.
2. Apply a small amount of nail glue directly to the underside of the artificial nail *and* to your own nails.
3. Press artificial nail firmly onto your own nail.
4. Trim the nail to a manageable length.
5. Shape the overnight with an emery board.
6. If artificial nails were purchased unpolished, apply color after they are secure.

When you want to remove the nails—they won't last through too much activity—use an orange-wood stick to pry them loose. They will pop off with little effort. Store them away for the next special occasion. Nail polish

remover will rid your nails of any glue residue. Although your nails will be well protected by the clear polish, apply some oil to them to restore moisture. Follow with a good basic manicure.

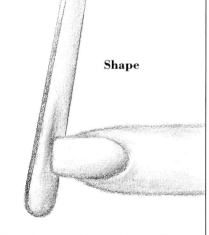

Shape

ACETATE TIPS   For do-it-yourselfers, I recommend acetate nail tips for lengthening one or more nails. They look and feel like they are your own nails and form the base from which you can choose a variety of shapes, lengths, and coverings. These tips are available in many stores that sell nail-care products. A package contains an assortment of sizes and widths to fit all nails. Wrapped in silk, as described earlier, or dipped into acrylic powder, they are strong and long-lasting.

It is not difficult to apply the tips. Beginning with a naked nail, follow these directions:

1. Gently smooth the nail top with your buffing disc.
2. Choose a tip that fits the width of the nail from corner to corner. If none gives a precise fit, use a larger one and trim the sides before attaching it to the nail.

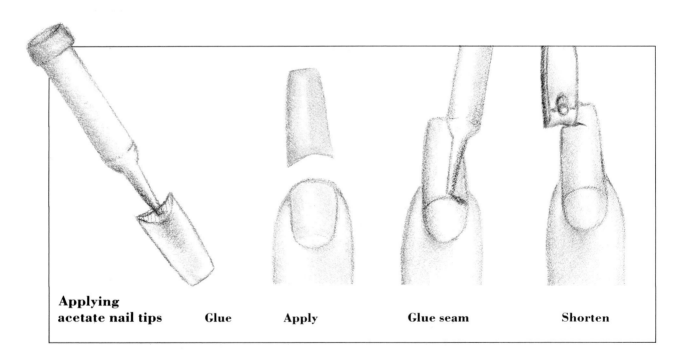

Applying acetate nail tips   **Glue**   **Apply**   **Glue seam**   **Shorten**

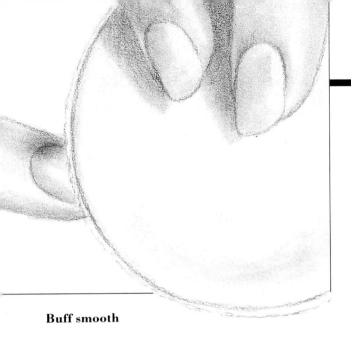
Buff smooth

SPECIAL TIP: Do not follow any of the procedures using glue if your nails or cuticles are sore, inflamed, or infected. If you simply *must* do something about your nails, use the overnights with the adhesive tabs, but keep them reasonably short so they are less likely to pop off.

3. Apply glue to the underside of the overlap ridge of the artificial nail tip.

4. Apply the tip to your nail, pressing it firmly. Hold it in place for a few seconds until the glue dries.

5. Apply glue to the top of the acetate tip (be sure to put a few drops on the seam where the tip and the natural nail meet). Allow it to dry.

6. With a toenail clipper, trim the nail tip to the desired length.

7. Finish shaping using your black emery board.

8. With your buffing disc, smooth the top of the nail tip and the area where the tip joins the natural nail.

9. Apply the fabric wrap (as described on pages 48–49) or dip the nail in acrylic, as described on the following page. If you wear the tips without this added protection they will pop off, break, or lose their shape in hot water. The fiber wrap or acrylic powder gives the nails extra strength and body, to hold their shape and retain polish.

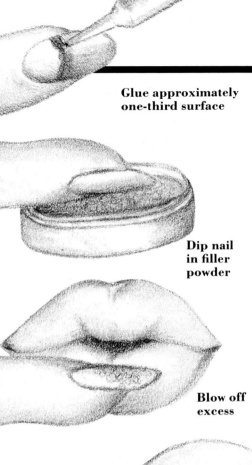

**Glue approximately
one-third surface**

**Dip nail
in filler
powder**

**Blow off
excess**

The directions that come with some acetate tips suggest that you apply glue to the top of the nail tips, then sprinkle the tips with thin coats of the filler. For greater ease in application, and a more thorough coating I prefer the following:

1. After the nail tips are firmly in place, and cut and filed to size, spread a few drops of glue over the tops. Be sure to cover the area where tip and nail join. (Don't worry if some glue gets on your own nail.)

2. Before glue dries, dip the tops of fingernails, one at a time, into a small container of acrylic filler powder.

3. Shake or blow off the excess powder.

4. Repeat the process three to four times.

5. With your buffing disc, buff off any excess filler powder.

6. Put one more coat of glue over the entire top of nail. Allow it to dry.

7. Buff again until smooth.

8. Apply ridge filler base coat, two coats of polish, and top coat.

SPECIAL TIP: Consider acetate tips before a two-week vacation. Your nails will look beautiful, and polish will adhere until after you have returned, unpacked, and are back at work. Take along extra tips, glue, and polish— just in case—but it's unlikely that you will need them.

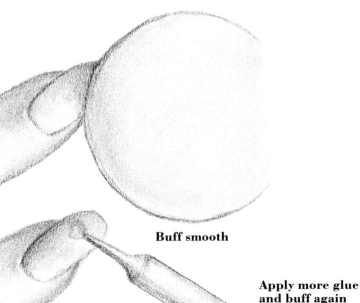

Buff smooth

**Apply more glue
and buff again**

Use only nonacetone polish remover on acetate nail tips. When you want to remove the tips, cut the length back with a clipper until you reach your natural nail. Then buff the top until you see your natural nail. You can soak tips in nail glue remover (available where you buy nail glue) or nail polish remover, but, as you know, this is very drying to the nails.

SCULPTURED NAILS

Sometimes called acrylic or artificial nails, sculptured nails look as beautiful a week after they are applied as they did the first day. That's because polish adheres like glue to the acrylic, so it never chips. But this is not a procedure to be performed by an amateur manicurist, however talented, and the nails require careful maintenance.

Go to a salon whose reputation has been established, and look around carefully. If you feel satisfied that it meets your personal standards of cleanliness, make an appointment. Don't try to fit it into a lunch hour and don't plan this first appointment just before a holiday when the manicurist may be overbooked. Allow at least one hour for a full set of sculptured nails, and plan to spend between $50 and $100. Expect to have weekly or biweekly maintenance appointments for fill-ins and cracks at a cost of $15 to $50. This maintenance is important, not just for cosmetic reasons, but to prevent moisture and dirt from becoming trapped under the artificial nail. A manicurist will take note (and I hope

you will too) if any bacteria or fungus has begun to grow. (An antifungal liquid should have been brushed on your bare nails before the acrylic was applied, to prevent fungus from being sealed in.) It is also worth noting that sculptured nails do not take kindly to creams and oils, or long soaks in the tub or pool; they will loosen. They are also inflammable.

There are two ways to build or brush on an acrylic nail. In one method, a form (which is removed when the acrylic dries) is placed snugly under the free edge of the nails and around the sides and the new nail is built out beyond the natural nail. In another method, acetate tips are first glued to the nails as a base for the acrylic. Either way, a brush is next dipped into a special liquid and then into an acrylic powder, forming a small lumpy ball of acrylic mix. This little ball is then placed on the base of the nail (some people prefer to start at the free edge working backward) to begin the sculpturing. The procedure continues until the nail and extension are completely covered. New strong nails are created, the edges of which are then shaped with an emery board designed for acrylic nails. The sculptured extension and the nail bed are buffed until smooth, and a ridge filler base coat, polish, and top coat are applied.

Remove sculptured nails as you would acetate tips. Clip the free edge back to the natural nail. With a buffing disc, buff the tops of nails until the acrylic is removed. You can also use a solvent made for this purpose. These sculptured nails should be removed every two months, although some people keep them for months and months at a time, usually destroying their own nails. Give your nails a few days of "freedom" at which time you treat them to some warm oil treatments to restore the moisture that the acrylic has removed.

Variations on the acrylic sculptured nails are continually being developed. For instance, gel nails have become popular in some salons. Gel needs the support of an acetate tip (in contrast to acrylic, which doesn't require that support). The gel, which is purchased already mixed in a bottle, is applied like nail polish with an acrylic or nylon brush. Then, in a process called *bonding*, the fin-

gers are placed under a special ultraviolet curing light, which bonds the gel to the nail. These lights represent a significant investment —anywhere from $150 to $700—(the better ones are at the top of the price range) and so are impractical for home use.

There are also some gels that don't require the bonding light; this product is similar to, and used like, acrylic. Polish adheres extremely well to these bonded gel nails but plan on regular visits to the salon, for they need fill-ins as your own nail grows. Remove gel or bonded nails the same way you remove acrylic nails.

NO MORE NAIL BITING

Nail biters come in all ages and sizes and neither gender has a monopoly on the habit. Unkempt and ragged hands can be a great source of embarrassment, and a nail biter may be perceived as anxiety-ridden instead of simply as someone with a bad habit.

In addition to the negative impressions generated, the nail biter or picker is constantly exposed to bacteria. Just think of all the things you touch: money, doorknobs, telephones, and car handles. Now envision this bacteria being transported from your fingers to your mouth. And nail biting often causes hangnails, which can result in infections.

Nail biters get themselves into a vicious cycle. First they bite their nails, then they can't stand the feeling of rough edges on nails and cuticles, so they bite some more.

Ready to break the habit? Read on.

1. Apply a cuticle softener and give yourself a fifteen-minute soap-and-water soak (longer than the standard five-minute one). This will help to soften those extra tough cuticles.

2. Push the cuticles back. Although I generally disapprove of cutting cuticles, the nail biter may have to trim those cuticles (with sanitized nippers) if they are excessively overgrown. These ragged cuticles are a great temptation to bite or pick at —and most nail biters do not just confine themselves to the free edge of the nail. Only a steady-handed experienced friend or a professional manicurist should trim cuticles. After this, you should be able to manage the cuticles yourself as described in chapter 5.

3. Use a buffing disc to file over any rough edges on top of the nail and at the free edge.

4. Moisturize the nails and cuticles with a good cream or petroleum jelly. Use it every time you wash your hands, and keep a small container or tube in your bag, briefcase, and desk drawer so that you can give yourself a few extra helpings during the day. Keep some in the kitchen and every bathroom and place one next to your bed so you are sure to rub it in before you turn off the lights. Keep buffing discs handy so that when you feel a rough edge you can take care of it immediately.

5. Give yourself a full manicure every three or four days for two months to eliminate all rough edges. By that time your nails will be well groomed—and although you may not look like a hand model you will be on your way!

6. Clear polish is required: It minimizes the temptation to bite. (Men can use matte finish, if they prefer.) Bad-tasting polish is also available at drugstores; this old-fashioned method still works for children, men, and women as an aversive type of behavior modification.

SPECIAL TIP: Parents may be reluctant to put polish on the nails of a very young nail biter, but don't skip this step; polish helps seal the layers of bitten nails, which tend to peel. Substitute matte finish polish for colored polish if you prefer.

Several years ago I patented a process that works well for curing nail biting in those who had tried a number of different methods with no success. It requires more time and effort than the procedure described above, but if you are having trouble breaking the habit I think you will find the following method will work for you, too.

1. Soak hands for fifteen minutes in warm soapy water.
2. Push back the cuticles with an orangewood stick, and trim with sterilized nippers (be sure someone experienced does this!) so they are not ragged.
3. Lightly buff the free edge and the top of the nail with a soft buffing disc to smooth out the surface.

4. Apply one drop of glue to the nail tip (avoid getting glue on the skin).
5. Apply an acetate tip to your nail. (You may have to place it close to the nail bed if your nail is very short.)
6. Apply another drop of glue where the tip joins the nail.
7. Using nail clippers, cut the acetate tip short. (When your own nails don't reach to or extend beyond the fingertips, long tips are more likely to break from slight pressure.)
8. Smooth the tip and shape oval or soft square (see page 24).

Applying a nail tip for nail biters

9. Apply glue carefully to the entire surface of the tip and natural nail. Avoid cuticles and sides of nail near the skin.

10. While the glue is still wet, dip your fingernail into small jar of acrylic filler powder (see page 56).

11. Shake or blow away excess filler powder.

12. Glue again, dip again, and blow away excess.

13. Glue again and allow to dry completely.

14. Buff entire nail, first with black emery board and then with buffing disc. Continue until nails are completely smooth.

SPECIAL TIP: If you have any small nicks or cuts around the cuticle, wait until they have healed before applying an acetate tip, because the glue used to adhere the tips can irritate open wounds.

15. Apply clear or colored polish.

These nails should last one to two months. If they begin to lift near the cuticles, reglue and buff them until they are smooth. And trim the tips as your own nails grow; it is better to keep them fairly short until you are used to having nails.

At the end of six weeks you will see the real growth of your own nails—and you will have broken the nail-biting habit.

Although this method is more appealing to women, it can be used very successfully by men. Simply keep nails short and squared, and use just one coat of a matte-finish polish.

Repairs and regrowth are possible for everyone. All it requires is the desire to do something about it, and the willingness to make the effort.

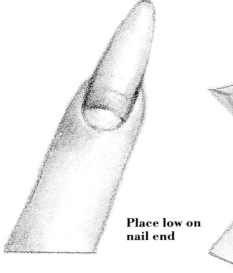

Place low on nail end

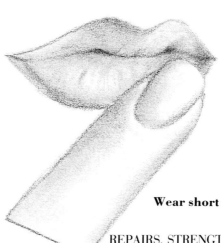

Wear short

7 FABULOUS FEET

Don't wait until you're packed for a winter cruise or Memorial Day weekend to give your feet the attention they deserve. Pretty painted toes are sexy all year round—and well-groomed toenails will prevent painful ingrown nails and save money on torn pantyhose. Although there are some differences, a pedicure is basically a manicure for the feet. In one sense it is even easier than giving yourself a manicure because you can use your dominant hand throughout the procedure.

HEALTHY FEET

Pretty feet begin with healthy feet. Shoes that fit properly, used for the purposes for which they are intended, and kept in good condition, can be the best friends your feet will ever have. Socks or hose should allow for toe-wiggling space, and should be changed daily, then washed and rinsed thoroughly. Walking on clean sand is good exercise for your feet but generally, walking around outside barefoot is *not* good for your feet; you are more likely to cut them or pick up fungus or bacte-

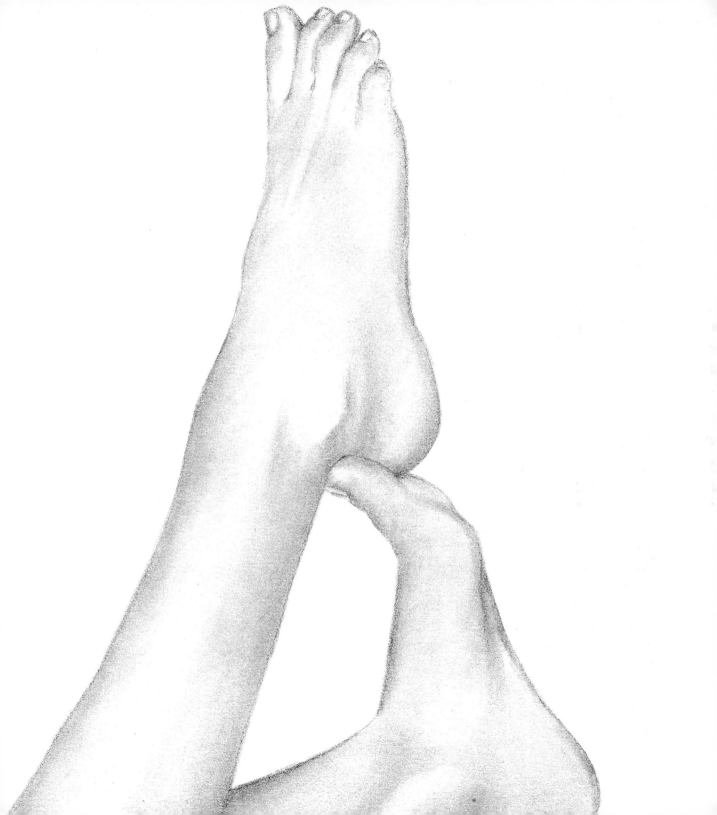

ria. Wear rubber or plastic sandals around the health club, in poolside showers, and in other places where you might pick up someone else's problems. Don't borrow or lend shoes or sneakers.

Feet should be washed daily with soap and water and dried thoroughly. Dry carefully (pat, and don't use a coarse towel) between the toes; in warm weather, or if you perspire a great deal, use cornstarch or foot powder. If your skin is very dry, apply a good moisturizing cream twice a day.

Burning feet can be annoying. Shoes or hose made of synthetic materials or other materials that don't breathe are usually the culprits. These same synthetic materials that seal moisture inside the shoe are closely identified with the onset of athlete's foot. Sometimes itching, peeling, or swelling are allergic reactions. Try applying cool, wet dressings, drying feet well, and changing to different shoes. If you have a tendency to athlete's

foot or other fungal infections, use specially formulated powder for that purpose. Occasionally, these problems have an underlying medical cause.

Diabetics need to take special precautions; those with ingrown toenails, corns, calluses, bunions, blisters, and warts need specific attention. See page 71 for further information.

BASIC FOOT HYGIENE

Basic hygiene should prevent foot odors; if it doesn't, you may need to take special measures. Most foot odor is caused by the bacteria in perspiration; sometimes by fungus. If regular washing and drying doesn't solve the problem, try an antiperspirant lotion, spray, or powder meant for feet and shoes.

Excessive perspiration keeps feet wet and makes you prone to rashes, infections, and even athlete's foot.

Leather is your best bet for shoes, because it is absorbent and allows perspiration to evaporate. Let shoes dry out for at least twelve, but preferably twenty-four hours between wearings. You can also replace synthetic sneaker and shoe liners with leather ones. Odor-destroying insoles for shoes and sneakers are also useful. Whenever possible wear socks; a combination of cotton or wool with synthetic fibers is the most effective against odor from perspiration. Toss those old sneakers in the washing machine, and any footwear that won't relinquish odor should be thrown away. If the problem persists, consult a physician. Occasionally a medical condition contributes to excessive perspiration.

Your regular hygiene routine should include a careful look at your feet; don't wait until they hurt to try to find out if there's a problem. End-of-day aching feet will often feel better after soaking in warm water to which epsom salts have been added; followed by a cool soak. Rub your feet with alcohol (or some pleasant cosmetic product made for this purpose) and give them a soothing massage with lotion.

ROUTINE CARE OF YOUR FEET

Twice a week check your toenails to see if they are ragged or have any rough edges that can tear hose. If necessary, smooth them with the buffing disc you use on your fingernails. Use your heavy emery board or pumice to rub off any dry skin or calluses and apply a good creamy lotion on the tops and bottoms of your feet.

Once a week, more often in wintertime, put a strong cream (lanolin, if you're not allergic) on your feet after an evening bath or shower. Sleep in an old pair of socks to protect bedsheets. Your feet will soon begin to look and feel smoother.

PRETTY PEDICURES

Toenails grow fastest in warm weather, and are more likely to be exposed during these months. A pedicure every two weeks should keep them in beautiful shape. Closed-toe shoes and indoor weather will offer your toes more protection so you can wait three to four weeks between pedicures the rest of the year.

SPECIAL TIP: Remember to give yourself a pedicure *before* you do your manicure; you don't want to smudge your finished nails.

One of the major differences between a manicure and pedicure is the position in which you work. I like to sit on a small stool in the bathroom, leaning my back against the wall and propping my feet on the edge of the tub. Others find the kitchen is a good spot. Sit on one kitchen chair, prop your feet on another one, or on your kitchen stool or stepladder. You may even prefer sitting on the floor, with your feet comfortably raised. Be sure you have good support for your back to avoid a backache the next day. Place your supplies conveniently within reach and make sure you have good lighting. And avoid drafts from fans, air-conditioners, or heaters.

STEP-BY-STEP TO A PERFECT PEDICURE

Fill the basin with warm, sudsy water, and add a drop of your favorite cologne or bath oil if you like. Settle yourself comfortably, and follow these steps:

STEP 1: REMOVE POLISH

Using cotton rolled into balls, and saturated with polish remover, loosen polish, then remove completely with an unsoiled area of the cotton. Rub away from the base to avoid getting polish into cuticles.

STEP 2: CUT AND SHAPE THE NAILS

No options here—to avoid ingrown toenails, shape toenails straight across. If they are long, use your toenail clippers to trim them to the right length, making small clips to avoid splitting the toenail. The nails should not be so long that they touch the edges of your shoes, or cut into the skin of neighboring toes, and not so short that they fail to offer the tips of your toes some protection. After clipping, buff edges perfectly smooth.

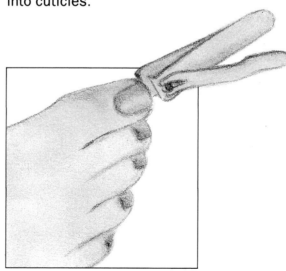

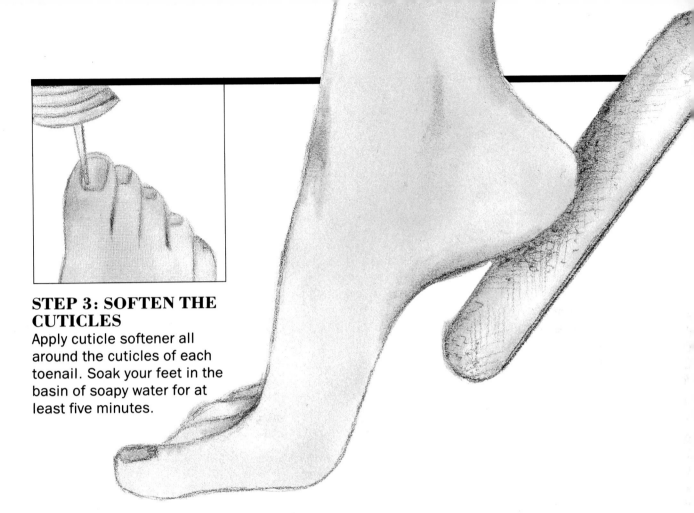

STEP 3: SOFTEN THE CUTICLES

Apply cuticle softener all around the cuticles of each toenail. Soak your feet in the basin of soapy water for at least five minutes.

Now, using the flat end of the orangewood stick, gently push back the cuticles of your nails. Trim any hangnails with your sanitized nippers. Dry feet well.

SPECIAL TIP: Give yourself a pedicure right after a bath. Your feet will get the same good soak and you will have accomplished two things at once!

STEP 4: SMOOTH YOUR FEET

Using a slougher, or a heavy-duty emery board, scraper, or pumice, rub off dead skin and work on any calluses.

STEP 5: MASSAGE FEET

Few things feel better than a foot massage. Not only can it relieve the weariness of too many hours on your feet, it can make you feel completely relaxed.

Here's how to give a foot massage—to yourself or someone else.

1. Apply cream all over the feet. Starting with both hands on the top of the foot, make rotary movements with the thumbs from the top of the instep down to the toes. Repeat three times. Now do the same thing around the sides of the foot, starting at the heel and working toward the toes. Repeat three times.

2. Put more cream on the feet, then with the thumb on the top, and two fingers on the bottom of the big toe, rotate thumb and fingers all over toe and nail. Repeat twice. Continue on the remaining toes.

3. Wrap your hand around your ankle, gently rotating it. Then, holding the ankle firmly, spread and close toes, lifting them up and down and wiggling them.

4. Still holding your ankle, apply the heel of the other hand to the ball of your foot and make rotating movements. Repeat three times.

5. Hold all your toes in one hand, gently lifting them up and down.

6. Hold the heel of your foot in your hand, and with the other hand rotate one toe at a time, repeating twice.

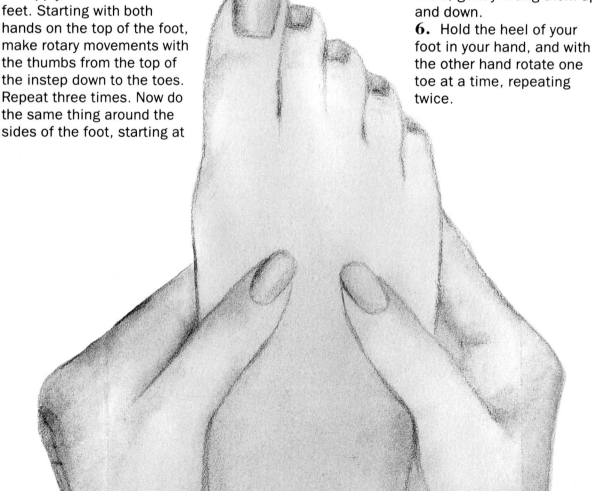

STEP 6: CLEANUP

Empty your basin and fill it with clean water, splashed with some cologne. Rinse each foot. (If you prefer, rinse feet under the bathtub faucet.) Dry your feet carefully with the towel, and remove all traces of cream from the nails with tissue dipped in polish remover. Splash feet with astringent (or cologne); allow them to dry.

STEP 7: BUFF

Buffing is a very attractive alternative to polish for the toenails, and many women prefer it, particularly in the winter. To buff, apply a dab of buffing paste to each toe with your fingertip. Stroking in one direction (base to nail edge or side to side), buff the nails with the buffer until they shine. Be sure to lift the buffer with each stroke or your nails will get very hot.

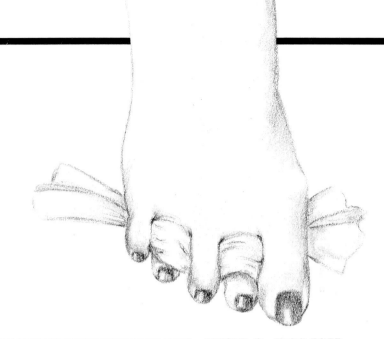

SPECIAL TIP: Men shouldn't wear polish on their toenails; it looks foolish. Leave toenails natural or buff them.

STEP 8: APPLY BASE COAT

Insert foam separators or weave tissues between toes to prevent polish from smearing onto adjacent toes. Then apply a ridge filler or other base coat. This will help the polish go on more smoothly, adhere better, and prevent your toenails from becoming stained.

STEP 9: POLISH

Give the polish a vigorous shake, then allow the bubbles to settle before using it. Be sure to wipe the upper side of the brush against the inside of the neck of the bottle so that you don't have too much polish on the brush.

If you are right-handed, begin with the small toe of the left foot, working toward the big toe. When you do the right foot, start with the largest toe. The converse applies if you are left-handed. This method avoids reaching across wet nails as you proceed.

Apply the polish as you do for a manicure: three (four, if your toenails are very wide) strokes; one (or two) down the center, then one down each side.

After two or three minutes, give your toenails another coat of polish. Allow five minutes of drying time before applying a top coat.

STEP 10: TOP COAT

A top coat, or a coat of clear polish, will give your toenails more protection and a nice glossy appearance.

STEP 11: OIL FINISH

Apply baby or kitchen oil, or a brush-on oil-finish product to your nails to help speed drying time.

Leave separators between toes for at least another fifteen minutes. Don't put on hose or shoes for another hour. Give yourself another hour still before going to bed.

SPECIAL TIP: The pedicure procedure is the same if you do yourself or a friend. It's a nice project for two; give each of you clean water, and be sure to dip the implements into alcohol between uses.

KEEPING YOUR PEDICURE FRESH

Apply a coat of clear polish every three or four days, allowing ten to fifteen minutes to dry. If a nail chips slightly, buff it with an emery board, then paint the chip with fresh polish. Allow to dry, then apply a coat of clear polish. If it is badly chipped, slip on the nail separator (or use tissues between toes), remove polish from the chipped nail, and reapply base coat and polish. (Protect your manicure by wearing rubber gloves when you use remover.)

WHEN TO SEE A PODIATRIST

If you have any foot problems that are not easily treated with self-care methods you should regularly see an experienced and reliable podiatrist. These health professionals have training from an accredited college of podiatry where they earn the degree of Doctor of Podiatric Medicine (DPM). The most highly trained are certified by the American Board of Podiatric Surgery and most are members of the American Podiatric Medical Association. They are licensed to treat medically, biomechanically, and surgically any injuries, deformities, skin conditions, and bone and joint problems of the feet. Family doctors, orthopedists, and dermatologists also often treat conditions of the feet.

SPECIAL PRECAUTIONS FOR DIABETICS

Diabetics, for whom injuries and infections of the feet are potentially dangerous, should pay special attention to their feet. They should wear cotton or wool socks, avoid any constricting hose or shoes, and should not go barefoot. A diabetic should not cut his or her own toenails (an emery board is usually fine) without first consulting a physician. Diabetics are usually cautioned against using corn pads, peroxide, epsom salts, boric acid, extreme temperatures, or any strong antiseptics.

People, especially diabetics, who notice any changes in the coloration or skin texture of the feet, or unusual swelling or pain should get off their feet and bring the condition to the attention of the family doctor or a podiatrist.

ATHLETE'S FOOT

Cracking, softening of skin, or redness between toes may signal the onset of athlete's foot, more correctly known as *tinea pedis*. The signs of athlete's foot are fluid-filled blisters on the soles or sides of the feet or in between toes. When caught early this usually can be treated with nonprescrip-

tion medications. If you don't see improvement in a few weeks, or if it worsens and you develop redness or swelling; dry, scaly tissues; or thick, white skin between the toes, see a dermatologist or podiatrist, who can determine if you have athlete's foot, or a look-alike inflammation like eczema, psoriasis, or a yeast infection. Ignoring athlete's foot can lead to complications; if skin is broken the infection can spread through the body. There are some excellent new prescription medications—including an oral one—for treating athlete's foot. Other conditions can also be treated effectively.

Some itchy, painful, or red conditions on feet may be contact dermatitis, which is simply an allergic reaction.

Try eliminating any new cosmetic, soap, or shoes to see if one of these things has caused the problem. It is possible suddenly to become allergic to something that you have used for a long time. See a dermatologist or podiatrist if it doesn't clear up soon.

INGROWN TOENAILS

If you have pressure, pain, redness, or swelling around the nail bed, or you can see the side of the nail cutting into the surrounding skin, it is probable that you have an ingrown toenail. Improper toenail clipping, extending too far into corners, can cause this. Picking at, ripping, or (heaven forbid!) biting toenails can all contribute to this condition.

Although there are home remedies, you would be wise to consult a podiatrist or orthopedist for evaluation and treatment, and then follow that doctor's advice for further care.

Until you see the doctor, soak your foot three times a day for twenty minutes in some warm water to which you have added one tablespoon of salt per quart. Then apply a nonprescription antibiotic cream and a bandage or place a bit of sterile cotton or gauze between the nail edge and the skin.

Do *not* cut a **V** in the center of the nail; this is an old myth that will not help and can cause more serious problems.

CORNS AND CALLUSES

Corns are little circular lumps composed of layers of dead cells, usually on the side of the small toe, on the top of a toe, or in between toes. They result from some kind of friction or pressure on the toes, often by shoes that are pressing down on the toes. A structural imbalance of bones or muscles may make you predisposed to corns. Home remedies abound but medications that contain acids can destroy healthy surrounding tissue as well as the corn. Instead, put some oil on the corn and soak your feet in warm water and rub gently with a mild abrasive like a buffpuff or loofah sponge, instead of pumice. Chances are, however, it will grow back, so a visit to a podiatrist will give you speedier and more lasting comfort.

Calluses, like corns, develop from pressure or friction. They usually start as a painless thickening of the skin on the ball of the foot or the heel where there is some pressure or friction. Too tight *or* too loose shoes can cause this but are not the chief offenders. People differ in foot structure in that some individuals can absorb the shocks of walking on pavements better than others. At the first onset of a callus, use pumice stone or a slougher made especially for this purpose. They help to roll off rough, dry skin.

Corns and calluses also can be softened by a twenty minute soak in soapy water. If a callus causes pain, is hot or red, or doesn't respond to home treatment, see a podiatrist. Deep root calluses must be removed professionally.

BUNIONS

An enlargement of the joint at the base of the great toe or little toe joint is called a bunion. A tendency toward bunions runs in families, because of its relationship to the structure of the foot. But chronic irritation and pressure, often from shoes that don't fit properly, will aggravate any small bunions. Bunions should be evaluated by a podiatrist, who can advise you how to avoid their growth and can treat any existing ones.

OTHER PROBLEMS

A painful, injured toenail, especially if it turns black and blue from collected blood, should be seen by a podiatrist or orthopedist in order to relieve the pressure.

Blisters are a direct result of irritation from an ill-fitting shoe, or, as your mother warned you, wearing sneakers without socks. If a blister develops, clean with alcohol, gently puncture with a sterile needle, then put an anti-biotic on it and cover with a bandage.

Veruccas, more often known as plantar warts, can develop anywhere on the foot. They look like thick calluses but should only be removed by a physician or podiatrist. Don't neglect them, because they can spread elsewhere.

Treat your feet kindly; nothing can lower your morale and make you look more tired than sore feet. See a podiatrist for problems that you can't solve yourself. Gazing down at attractive, happy feet can raise your spirits and make you feel as if you are walking on air, and make even those sensible comfortable sandals look like designer shoes.

SOMETHING
SPECIAL

8 By now, I'm sure you have banished forever the belief that manicures are only for "the ladies who lunch." Everyone can, and should, manicure their nails. And that includes teens, women who work in the home, grand-mothers who baby-sit, and great-grand-mothers who care as much about their appearance as they ever did—as well as women who work outside of the home. *And*, it also includes men. A man needs more than a clipper and scrub brush; his manicure should be as much a part of his grooming routine as shampoos, haircuts, and shaves.

Sometimes a special manicure is called for: brides, for instance, may want to try something different. And it's fun to use your imagination on those occasions that call for a little excitement and special effects.

HOLIDAY FUN

If you're younger than sixteen or over eighteen, decals and crazy designs look absurd—most of the time. But I can't think of anything more fun than spelling out HAPPY B'DAY on your nails when you're the hostess at a surprise party.

A few little Christmas trees are amusing for a holiday party, and Halloween simply cries out for some clever decal design. Red, white, and blue stripes with a few stars thrown in for good measure are perfect when you're hosting a Fourth of July bash. You get the message: decals and designs are not going to make you look like the serious woman you are Monday through Friday but are splendid for special occasions.

With a steady hand and the right materials, you can achieve any effect you like. Just keep in mind that there is a time and place for everything and grownup people shouldn't show up for work—unless they are in a highly creative field—with anything but neatly groomed and attractively polished or buffed nails of reasonable length.

NAIL SHADING

Nail shading is one new look that you can achieve easily at home. Start with a half-filled bottle of very bright pink or red nail polish. Polish both your pinkies with this color. Then add a few drops of white polish to your bottle and shake well. Apply this lighter shade to the nails of both ring fingers. Add a few more drops of white, making the polish lighter and shake well. Apply to both middle fingers. Continue this process until the lightest shade is on your thumb.

Many cosmetic counters carry a wide array of materials for creating special nail effects, or you can order from some of the professional sources listed on page 86. Nail pens, for instance, are very much like magic markers and come in just as many colors, including gold and silver. You can draw simple designs such as stripes or polka dots on your nails, or you can be as creative as your talents permit.

Stick-ons are easier still to use, and they come in stripes of varying widths and colors (everything from primary colors, some solid and some transparent with white or colored borders, to silver, gold, and rainbow glitters), as well as a big selection of designs, including sparkling "jewels." You simply place them on the nail and, if you are using a strip, cut off at the edge, then file the end off for the precise length and a tighter bond. After the stick-on is in place, follow with two coats of clear polish or top coat.

The newest rage in nail painting today is graphic designs achieved by air brushing (something like a fine-grain spray paint, but requiring expensive

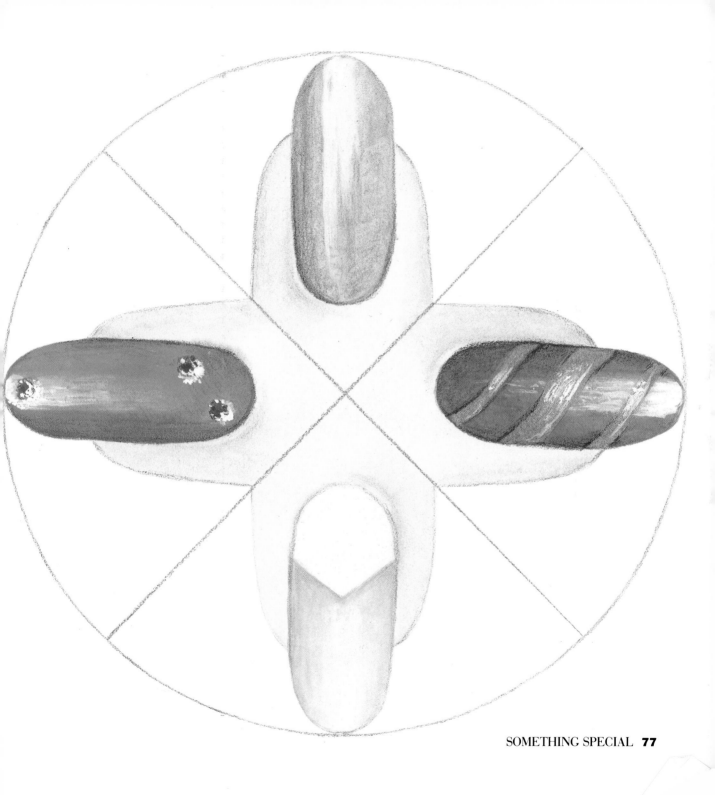

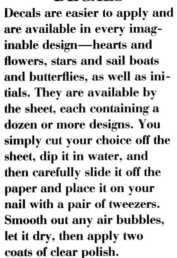

APPLYING DECALS

Decals are easier to apply and are available in every imaginable design—hearts and flowers, stars and sail boats and butterflies, as well as initials. They are available by the sheet, each containing a dozen or more designs. You simply cut your choice off the sheet, dip it in water, and then carefully slide it off the paper and place it on your nail with a pair of tweezers. Smooth out any air bubbles, let it dry, then apply two coats of clear polish.

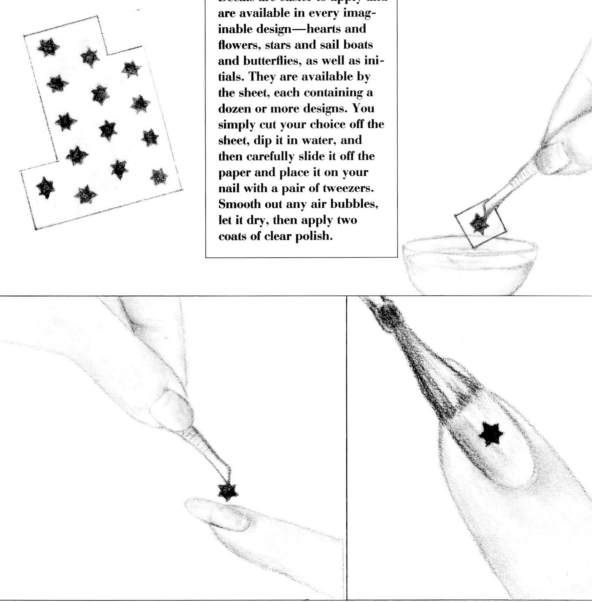

machinery) with stencils. With a little practice, this is even easier (and more reliable) than painting freehand designs, which is why a growing number of salons offer this service. It is also used for doing French manicures. Airbrushing is best left to those salons who have invested in the equipment.

The glitziest look of all is gold, jeweled, or feathered nails that are glued over your own nail. You can use an entire matching (or unmatched!) set, or confine the effect to one finger. They come in every shape and size—even for toenails! Initials, ornaments, and small precious stones can be set into a jeweled nail or an artificial nail tip. A hole is drilled through the nail tip, and the nail jewel is placed in it somewhat like a pierced earring. Thus, the jewels can be later applied to other artificial nails.

One stunning woman I know—a department store executive whose husband is a financial analyst—has a diamond (yes, a real one!)

screwed into her sculptured nail. But if you opt for this look, use your hands very carefully so you won't lose your investment and be sure to wear cotton gloves when you get dressed so you don't get snags and tears in your hose and hand-knits.

Small gold (or gold-tone) charms ranging from music notes to hearts and tennis rackets can be securely glued to artificial nails for a festive look.

You can do many of these designs on your toes. An effective and festive look can be achieved by setting one small flat rhinestone on

SPECIAL TIP: For a splashy occasion you can duplicate the look of jeweled nails with a little more subtlety. Simply apply a splash of inexpensive rhinestones, sparkles, glitter, or stars (available in arts and crafts stores) to the nail of your pinky or index finger while the polish is still wet—then after they have dried, follow with two coats of clear polish.

one of your toes for a pool party or before you go off on a cruise. A bold stripe or some other decal looks great on your big toe and is bound to get attention when you put your toes in the water.

Women have been adorning their hands and nails since Egyptian times. In India, women draw designs in henna on the palms of their hands, creating an intricate pattern in stain, which lasts a month or two. In Thailand women wear long metal curved nails to perform their native dances.

BABIES AND SMALL CHILDREN

Don't worry—I'm not advocating nail polish on toddlers, but I firmly believe that it is never too soon to care for babies' and children's fingernails. Nails that are too long or have rough edges can catch on toys and clothes, resulting in hangnails or painful breaks. Babies and young children can scratch themselves, especially in their sleep, so it is imperative that their nails be gently smoothed.

Use special safety baby scissors or a nail clipper sized especially for little fingers to cut off nails that extend beyond the fingertips. Don't use adult scissors or clippers—they are too large and heavy; using them can easily result in an accident. Follow with the buffing disc or smoothie (not an emery board), to smooth any

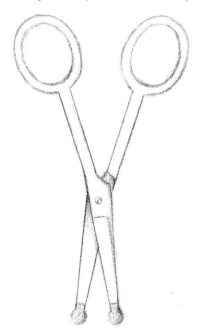

Baby scissors

remaining rough edges. For ease in handling, you can cut the smoothie down to a 3- or 4-inch size, or purchase gentle little nail shapers meant for babies and small children. Hold the shaper or smoothie at a slight angle to the nail and file from side to center. Be sure you don't saw back and forth.

Many children's fingernails need little or no attention—they seem to be so fragile that a nightly soak in the bathtub keeps the length in check. But examine your child's hands carefully—don't wait for a hangnail, which can easily become painful and infected, or a scratch across the cheek to discover that little people need hand care, too.

ADOLESCENTS

One minute they are small children, allowing you to "check them out" carefully, and the next minute they are adolescents who seem to come out of their rooms only to eat, meet their friends, or get their allowances. This is the time that you can start

them on the road to healthy and attractive nails. Buy your favorite teen his or her own basic tools, and put them in a carrying case so they don't disappear under the bed or in a desk drawer.

Give your youngster the first manicure, explaining the basic steps as you go along. Make it a really pleasurable experience, keeping instructions and materials to a minimum. Don't include sharp cuticle nippers; youngsters are likely to use them too enthusiastically. *You* cut any hangnails, using your own sanitized nippers.

THE ADOLESCENT GIRL A teenage girl will probably be delighted at the prospect of a manicure. Give her an attractive clear, flowery, or paisley carrying case for her supplies, and fill it with the following:
- fine-grain emery boards
- buffing disc
- orangewood stick
- nail brush
- chamois buffer
- buffing paste
- cotton
- nail polish remover
- cuticle softener

- ridge filler
- clear, sheer, nude, or pale pink polish (choice of two)
- clear top coat
- scented hand cream

Girls usually want attractive nails but are less than enthusiastic about the process and time needed to keep them so. The result: broken or chipped nails that look dreadful and can discourage even the most fastidious girl. For this reason, it is wise to keep goals realistic. Neat, short nails buffed, or with colorless or a pale shade of polish, look best on young teens, and are more likely to remain neat looking than nails that are long or brightly colored. For special occasions, suggest a French manicure. When you give her a pedicure or teach her to do it herself, use pale colors—pinks or corals. Young teens should not use nail glue to repair broken nails, or artificial nails to replace broken ones. The glue can be dangerous and few teens are dextrous enough to do an effective job. By midteens, they may want their nails a little longer, and if they have had a few years of practice in doing their own manicures, they may be ready for a more sophisticated look.

A young girl's manicure is much like that of an adult. (Refer to chapter 5 for step-by-step instructions on giving yourself a manicure.) Be sure her equipment is in good condition. Check that the polish hasn't thickened. If it has, lend her some of your solvent.

Start the manicure by suggesting she wash her hands well with a scrub brush, soap, and water. Then remove any old nail polish. Regardless of the shape of her hands or fingers, shape the nails in a rounded or oval shape and keep the length short. Soften the cuticle, and, if she has the patience, get her to soak her hands. If she's watching the clock, just send her back to wash her hands again. Then carefully push back the cuticles, reminding her to do it gently at least once a week. Give her a hand massage using hand cream (she may stop eyeing the clock for a while), and then another hand wash to remove any cream that's surrounding the nails or cuticle.

Follow with a good buffing. If she prefers polish, limit it to three coats: Use a ridge filler as a base coat, followed by one coat of nude or light polish, then one coat of clear top coat. Put on her favorite video, and have her sit for ten minutes. Then apply some oil to the nails to speed up the complete drying. By limiting a teen to only one coat of polish, you reduce drying time and she will be less likely to smudge her nails.

Remind her there are no faster ways to dry nails; hair dryers and heaters only make polish bubble. And tell her that most of those appealing nail gadgets are completely useless.

SPECIAL TIP: If you're nervous, or feel unsure about giving your teen that first manicure, let a professional do it. But don't make an appointment on a weekend when the salon is jammed.

THE ADOLESCENT BOY

A boy may initially be reluctant to have a manicure, but remind him that attractive men have well-groomed nails and that girls will notice his hands just as much as they notice his hair, to which he undoubtedly gives much thought and attention. Give him a masculine-looking case or even a shave-kit for his supplies. The case should include the following:

- nail brush
- fine-grain emery board
- buffing discs
- orangewood stick
- chamois buffer
- buffing paste (optional)
- cuticle softener
- hand cream

A boy should be encouraged to file his nails straight across, or slightly rounded on the edges, depending on the shape of his nail bed. Be sure not to file too close on the corners, or his nails will take on a feminine appearance. Give him a good soaping and scrubbing with a nail brush, then push back the cuticles with the orangewood stick. Clean under the nails, dry thoroughly, and buff with the chamois buffer twenty times in one direction. The use of buffing paste is optional—some young boys feel it makes their nails too shiny—but you can buff without it. Be sure to lift the buffer between strokes; the ensuing concentrated heat can be very uncomfortable. Then gently—and briefly—massage his hand with hand cream. Nothing too perfumed, please!

This ten-minute manicure is guaranteed not to try his patience, and will get him into a good habit. It's a good preventive for nail biters (it had that positive effect on my son), teaches them to be more conscious of hygiene, and looks and feels good!

One final admonition: *Never* put shiny clear polish on a teenage boy—it looks pretentious and tacky! Buff or use matte polish.

MANICURES FOR MEN

Don't ignore the man in your life. You can give yourselves manicures together—he can watch you and learn—or if you are feeling magnanimous, give him one before you do your own. A thoughtful gift would be his own manicure case, with a handmade certificate promising a weekly manicure. Pack his case with the following items for manicures and pedicures:

- emery boards
- orangewood stick
- nail brush
- toenail clippers
- cuticle nipper
- cuticle softener
- chamois buffer
- buffing paste
- unscented hand cream
- clear or matte finish nail polish (optional)

A great many men are self-conscious about going to a nail salon for a manicure or pedicure. They often prefer privacy, and are uncomfortable in the feminine atmosphere. Manicurists usually work only a part-time schedule at traditional barber shops, which may not coincide with his haircut appointment; besides, most men only get a haircut monthly. But hands need weekly attention. So once he recognizes his reluctance is not related to the manicure itself, you may get him to relax and enjoy it in the privacy of the home.

A man's manicure is much like a woman's. If his nails are very long when you give him his initial manicure, clip the nails with a nail clipper, then file into shape. File them straight across, rounding the edges slightly. If his nail base is round, then follow his natural shape. Men's nails should always be filed short, leaving very little free edge. However, nails that are too short, with no free edge showing, look unnatural. Filing the nails flush with the end of the fingertip is a good guideline.

SPECIAL TIP: Wonder how male models have such perfect nails? They run a metal pusher under the free edge, creating a perfect line, then apply a dampened white pencil under the nail. It looks great for pictures but disappears the first time he washes his hands.

Apply cuticle softener, soak in warm water, or treat him to a warm oil soak. Then push back the cuticle, just as you do in your own manicure. He should use a scrubbing brush to get rid of any imbedded dirt. Then give his hands a good massage; I guarantee he'll love it! Remove any excess cream and then buff his nails. Remember to apply a small dab of paste to the center of the nail and buff in one direction, approximately twenty-five to thirty strokes per nail. Be sure to lift the buffer so you don't burn his

A man's manicure

nails. Buffing increases circulation, encouraging growth, and gives nails a handsome, well-groomed appearance. Suggest he buff his nails once or twice a week between manicures.

Some men like clear polish on their nails. It tends to look a bit too shiny for my taste—I prefer buffing or a nail glaze available from some beauty suppliers that dries to a matte finish, looking a bit like frosted glass.

THE MATURE WOMAN

Remember that television commercial for dishwashing liquid in which the announcer challenged you to guess which hands belonged to the mother, and which to the daughter? Well, most mothers of grown daughters don't just naturally have youthful hands. Hands age faster than any other exposed area of the skin, including your face, because the skin contains few oil glands. But there's a lot you can do to keep them youthful and attractive.

Women complain most about age spots—those pigmentary changes that appear on hands (and faces), sometimes caused by thinning of the skin or too much sun. You can avoid getting "liver spots" by staying out of the sun or using a sun block with a sun protection factor (SPF) of 15 or higher.

If you already have age spots, there's no use lamenting those days you spent playing tennis or holding a book open in the sun. Try a nonprescription skin-bleaching cream, and you should begin to see some results before too long. You might want to discuss this with your dermatologist, who may prescribe something stronger. These spots can also be removed surgically; discuss with a dermatologist or plastic surgeon. A good solution is to use a cover stick and blend with your makeup. If you have excess hair on fingers or arms, use a depilatory, have them

<table>
<tr><td colspan="2">HOMEMADE BLEACH</td></tr>
</table>

HOMEMADE BLEACH
- **Combine in plastic bottle with narrow spout:**
2 ounces oil bleach
1 ounce 20-volume peroxide ⎱ available in pharmacies
- **Mix gently.**
- **Apply a thin layer to areas to be bleached. Leave for seven to ten minutes.**
- **Wash off thoroughly with soap.**
- **Moisturize skin with rich cream.**

waxed, or just bleach them. Take a patch test on a quarter-size area on the underside of the arm before bleaching. Use a commercial bleach according to directions or prepare your own.

If your hands are very dry, use a sloughing agent (a cream that contains an abrasive) meant for hands or feet. If you prefer, you can combine oatmeal and bran, and rub into your wet hands. Rinse, then moisturize your hands.

To keep hands looking young, wear a good moistur-

BRIDES' MANICURES

Just before the wedding, many brides seem to be drawn like magnets to a cosmetic counter where they spend a small fortune on things they never used before and will probably never use again.

When I work with brides I suggest they (and the groom) get used to the look they are planning before the big day. Start to grow your nails even *before* you order the invitations. That's the time to be conscientious about weekly manicures and using a liquid fiber wrap to strengthen them. If you don't meet with immediate success, then try a set of medium-length tips with silk wraps. Give yourself a chance to get used to the new nail and length. Practice putting on earrings, pulling up zippers, and doing all the everyday things that are vital to your functioning. If you break a nail (and most people do the first week) you still have time to practice repairing it so that you won't panic when you're on your honeymoon.

Choose a color wisely. Pearly whites, once the rage, aren't flattering to everyone. Too bright or deep a color is excessively dramatic on a bride's hands and presents too sharp a contrast to a white dress (as you will sadly discover when you look at your wedding pictures). Wear a nail color that is right for you; light or medium shades look best. You can choose from an array of pinks, pearly peaches, nearly nudes, and opalescents with a soft hint of color. Unless your skin tone is dark, the white polishes will offer no contrast at all to your dress and skin, and can make you look rather ghostly. You wouldn't wear white lipstick; don't wear white polish. Remember, your hands and nails should look picture-perfect to show off your brand-new wedding band.

chapter 5, and use extra cuticle creams and moisturizers to keep your nails supple.

Give yourself a weekly manicure, staying away from extremes of color and length. The dark reds and browns or whites are too harsh and draw attention to your hands. Tans and taupes are less flattering than true pinks or light reds. Clear polish may not be as becoming as it once was, because of new ridges and white spots. Use color judiciously. Extra-long nails are clumsy to use, and are unbecoming to the classic look you have developed.

Contemporary busy women know that having well-groomed hands and nails is another reflection of their own self-esteem. I believe that everyone should be the best they can, so I am pleased that now, *you* know how to achieve and how to keep the look you want.

izer under your gloves in the winter, and be scrupulous about remembering to wear protective gloves when handling detergents or other chemicals.

Nail growth slows down for many women in their later years and brittleness is often a problem. Indulge yourself with lactol or oil manicures, as described in

SOURCE LISTING

If you are unable to find any of the materials described in this book at your local variety or beauty and health supply store, the following sources can provide you with everything you need. And remember that catalog shopping by phone, mail, or through a representative at work or home may be the most efficient way to get just what you want.

Avon Products, Inc.
9 West 57 Street
New York, NY 10019
Shop at home or office through a representative, seeing samples and a catalog. Write to Avon at the above address or call (800) 858-8000 to request that a representative contact you.

The following suppliers will provide you with a catalog from which you can order supplies by mail.

Nail Emporium
606 West Katella
Orange, CA 92667
(714) 532-5566
(800) 624-5787
(800) 624-5777

Nail Supply Center
5521 East South Street
Lakewood, CA 90713
(800) 262-4421 in CA
(800) 356-2442 outside CA

SRA Nailady
69 Hampton Place
Freeport, NY 11520
(516) 378-4800

Nails at Last
674 Main Street
Hyannis, MA 02601
(617) 790-0027

The following offer a sharpening service by mail.

John's Sharpening Service
6301 Tenth Avenue
Brooklyn, NY 11219
(718) 680-4492

Tweezerman Corporation
Service Department
7601 Highway 12
Minneapolis, MN 55426
(612) 593-1245